"I wrote these songs in not a meditative state at all, but more like in a trancelike, hypnotic state. This is how I feel? Why do I feel like that? And who's the me that feels this way? I couldn't tell you that, either. But I know that those songs are just in my genes and I couldn't stop them comin' out."

Bob Dylan, 2006

Published by MJF Books
Fine Communications
322 Eighth Avenue
New York, NY 10001

Dylan
LC Control Number: 2011921616
ISBN-13: 978-1-60671-053-1
ISBN-10: 1-60671-053-2

Compiled by Chris Charlesworth
Text by Peter Doggett
Music and text edited by Ann Barkway and Andy Neill
Book design by Paul Tippett at Vitamin P

Photo research by Dave Brolan
Front Cover Photograph Copyright © by Jerry Schatzberg
Back Cover Photograph Copyright © by Barry Feinstein
Text photographs courtesy of Ted Russell/Eyevine – Pages 6, 15, 22, 35, 78-79
John Launois/Eyevine – Pages 10-11
Don Hunstein/Sony BMG Music Entertainment – Pages 18-19, 30, 74, 135, 160, 305, 474
Copyright © by Daniel Kramer – Pages 27, 38, 46-47, 56, 66-67, 82, 100, 106, 125, 140, 147,
    150, 155, 168
Douglas R. Gilbert/Redferns – Pages 43, 71, 88-89
Copyright © by Barry Feinstein – Pages 52, 172, 182-183, 186-187, 190, 196-197, 200, 207,
    210, 224, 248, 297, 317, 326, 410, 434, 458-459, 464
Copyright © by Jim Marshall – Pages 61, 117, 229
Copyright © by Tony Frank – Pages 92, 176-177 · Harry Goodwin – Page 97
Copyright © by Jerry Schatzberg – Pages 112, 120, 128-129, 164-165, 393, 452
Jan Persson/Redferns – Pages 216, 240 · Frank Dandridge/Alpha – Page 221
Copyright © by Ken Regan/Camera5 – Pages 232-233, 310, 323, 333, 336-337, 340, 353, 358,
    362, 367, 370, 386, 404-405, 481, 490
Elliott Landy/Redferns – Pages 236, 245, 257, 278 · Rex Features – Pages 252, 376, 429
Redferns – Pages 260, 300 · Corbis – Page 267 · Gettyimages – Pages 272, 285
Henry Diltz/Corbis – Page 290 · Copyright © by Joel Bernstein – Pages 346, 383, 440-441
Michael Putland/Retna – Page 398 · Ebet Roberts/Redferns – Pages 416-417
Aaron Rappaport/Retna – Page 422 · Deborah Feingold/Corbis – Page 447
Copyright © by Danny Clinch – Pages 468-469 · Lee Celano/Corbis – Page 481

This edition is published by MJF Books in arrangement with Music Sales Corporation.

Printed in China

MJF Books and the MJF colophon are trademarks of Fine Creative Media, Inc.

OGP   10 9 8 7 6 5 4 3 2 1

DYLAN

100 SONGS & PICTURES

MJF BOOKS

New York

CONTENTS

SONG TO WOODY

🎵 *Bob Dylan, 1962*

One of only two self-composed songs on Dylan's 1962 debut album, 'Song To Woody' was written in February 1961. It was a heartfelt tribute to the strongest influence on his early career, folk music pioneer Woody Guthrie. During his early months in New York, Dylan regularly visited Guthrie in hospital, where the veteran was suffering from Huntington's Chorea, and on at least one occasion he was able to play his hero this song.

"That's good, Bob. That's damned good."

Woody Guthrie's reaction to 'Song To Woody', 1961

"Woody likes me – he tells me to sing for him – he's the greatest holiest godliest one in the world."

Bob Dylan, postcard to a friend, 1961

SONG TO WOODY

2. Hey, hey Woody Guthrie, I wrote you a song
   'Bout a funny ol' world that's a-comin' along
   Seems sick an' it's hungry, it's tired an' it's torn
   It looks like it's a-dyin' an' it's hardly been born

3. Hey, Woody Guthrie, but I know that you know
   All the things that I'm a-sayin' an' a-many times more
   I'm a-singin' you the song, but I can't sing enough
   'Cause there's not many men that done the things that you've done

4. Here's to Cisco an' Sonny an' Leadbelly too
   An' to all the good people that traveled with you
   Here's to the hearts and the hands of the men
   That come with the dust and are gone with the wind

5. I'm a-leavin' tomorrow, but I could leave today
   Somewhere down the road someday
   The very last thing that I'd want to do
   Is to say I've been hittin' some hard travelin' too

BLOWIN' IN THE WIND

The Freewheelin' Bob Dylan, 1963

Perhaps the most enduring song to come out of the early 1960s folk scene, 'Blowin' In The Wind' became an anthem of the civil rights movement in America. It was composed around April 1962, debuted during Dylan's shows at Gerde's Folk City in New York's Greenwich Village, and recorded for posterity on *The Freewheelin' Bob Dylan* in July that year. Peter, Paul & Mary and Stevie Wonder both scored Top 10 hits with cover versions of the song.

"'Blowin' In The Wind' became the best-known anthem of social conscience throughout the world."

Joan Baez

"He was the real thing. I already knew about his talent, but he was obviously adding to his repertoire. These new songs were his own music."

Paul Stookey, Peter, Paul & Mary, on seeing Bob Dylan in 1962

BLOWIN' IN THE WIND

how man - y times must the can - non balls ___ fly Be -
how man - y times can a man turn his head, Pre -
how man - y deaths will it take till he knows That

fore they're ___ for - ev - er banned? _____
tend - ing he just does - n't see? _____
too man - y peo - ple have died? _____ The

an - swer, my friend, is blow-in' in the wind, The an - swer is

1. & 2.

3.

blow-in' in the wind. _____ wind. _____ The

Slower

an - swer is blow - in' _____ in the wind. _____

TOMORROW IS A LONG TIME

Bob Dylan's Greatest Hits, Vol. 2, 1971

Despite being written as early as 1962, this beautiful song did not appear on any of Dylan's early albums. Indeed, he did not release it until a vintage live tape appeared on his *More Greatest Hits* compilation. But it was tackled by many of his folk contemporaries, including Ian & Sylvia, Bud & Travis and Judy Collins. It was also the only Dylan song ever performed by Elvis Presley, a version which Dylan once quoted as his favourite ever interpretation of his material, and covered by Rod Stewart on the big selling 1971 album *Every Picture Tells A Story*.

TOMORROW IS A LONG TIME

Moderato rubato

1. If to-day was not an end-less high-way, ___ If to-night ___ was not a crook-ed
2. I can't see my reflec-tion in the wa-ters, ___ I can't speak ___ the sounds that show no
3. There's beauty in the sil-ver, sing-in' riv-er, ___ There's ___ beauty in the sun-rise in the

trail, If to-mor-row was-n't ___ such a long time, ___ Then
pain, I can't hear the ech-o ___ of my foot-steps, ___ Or
sky, But ___ *none of these, and nothing else can touch the beau-ty ___ That

Refrain

lone-some would mean noth-ing to you ___ at all. Yes, and on-ly if my own true love was
can't re-mem-ber the sound of my ___ own name.
I re-mem-ber in ___ my true love's eyes.

wait-in', ___ Yes, and if I could hear her heart a-soft-ly pound-in', ___

D.S.

On-ly if she was ly-in' by ___ me, ___ Then I'd lie in my bed once ___ a-gain.

* ad lib quasi recitative

"We all thought Bob was phenomenal. Songwriters love to hear good songs, and it really had the effect of spurring us to keep trying to improve our writing. It just happened that a lot of the good songs we heard were from Bob. The first time I heard Ian & Sylvia sing 'Tomorrow Is A Long Time', which is not a widely sung Dylan song, I remember thinking, 'That song is utterly beautiful'."

Tom Paxton

BALLAD OF HOLLIS BROWN

💿 *The Times They Are A-Changin'*, 1963

Written in the late summer of 1962, 'Ballad Of Hollis Brown' was recorded during the initial sessions for Dylan's third album, *The Times They Are A-Changin'*, in August 1963. His first known live performance of the song came almost a year earlier, during his debut performance at New York's Carnegie Hall.

"The songs are there. They exist by themselves, just waiting for someone to write them down. If I didn't do it, someone else would."

Bob Dylan, 1962

BALLAD OF HOLLIS BROWN

Moderato (in 4)

Em
(Em throughout)

Hol - lis Brown, He lived on the out - side of town, Hol - lis

Brown, He lived on the out - side of town, With his

wife and five chil - dren And his cab - in fall - in' down. ___

Refrain

1. You looked for work and mon - ey And you walked a rug - ged mile, ___

You looked for work and mon - ey And you walked a rug - ged mile. ___

Your chil - dren are so hun - gry That they

| 1-2-3 etc. (repeat for additional lyrics) | Last time |
| | *Fine* |

don't know how to smile. ___ 2. Your

2. Your baby's eyes look crazy
   They're a-tuggin' at your sleeve
   Your baby's eyes look crazy
   They're a-tuggin' at your sleeve
   You walk the floor and wonder why
   With every breath you breathe

3. The rats have got your flour
   Bad blood it got your mare
   The rats have got your flour
   Bad blood it got your mare
   If there's anyone that knows
   Is there anyone that cares?

4. You prayed to the Lord above
   Oh please send you a friend
   You prayed to the Lord above
   Oh please send you a friend
   Your empty pockets tell yuh
   That you ain't a-got no friend

5. Your babies are crying louder
   It's pounding on your brain
   Your babies are crying louder now
   It's pounding on your brain
   Your wife's screams are stabbin' you
   Like the dirty drivin' rain

6. Your grass it is turning black
   There's no water in your well
   Your grass is turning black
   There's no water in your well
   You spent your last lone dollar
   On seven shotgun shells

7. Way out in the wilderness
   A cold coyote calls
   Way out in the wilderness
   A cold coyote calls
   Your eyes fix on the shotgun
   That's hangin' on the wall

8. Your brain is a-bleedin'
   And your legs can't seem to stand
   Your brain is a-bleedin'
   And your legs can't seem to stand
   Your eyes fix on the shotgun
   That you're holdin' in your hand

9. There's seven breezes a-blowin'
   All around the cabin door
   There's seven breezes a-blowin'
   All around the cabin door
   Seven shots ring out
   Like the ocean's pounding roar

10. There's seven people dead
    On a South Dakota farm
    There's seven people dead
    On a South Dakota farm
    Somewhere in the distance
    There's seven new people born

A HARD RAIN'S A-GONNA FALL

The Freewheelin' Bob Dylan, 1963

This apocalyptic ballad entered Dylan's repertoire in September 1962, and was recorded for *The Freewheelin' Bob Dylan* three months later. It has rarely left his live repertoire since then, and has been performed as an electric rock song (during the mid-1970s Rolling Thunder Revue shows) and with an orchestra (at a 1994 festival in Japan).

"I wrote it at the time of the Cuban [missile] crisis. I was in Bleecker Street in New York. We just hung around at night – people sat around wondering if it was the end, and so did I… It was a song of desperation. What could we do? Could we control men on the verge of wiping us out? The words came fast, very fast."

Bob Dylan, 1965

A HARD RAIN'S A-GONNA FALL

2. Oh, what did you see, my blue-eyed son?
   Oh, what did you see, my darling young one?
   I saw a newborn baby with wild wolves all around it
   I saw a highway of diamonds with nobody on it
   I saw a black branch with blood that kept drippin'
   I saw a room full of men with their hammers a-bleedin'
   I saw a white ladder all covered with water
   I saw ten thousand talkers whose tongues were all broken
   I saw guns and sharp swords in the hands of young children
   And it's a hard, and it's a hard, it's a hard, it's a hard
   And it's a hard rain's a-gonna fall

3. And what did you hear, my blue-eyed son?
   And what did you hear, my darling young one?
   I heard the sound of a thunder, it roared out a warnin'
   Heard the roar of a wave that could drown the whole world
   Heard one hundred drummers whose hands were a-blazin'
   Heard ten thousand whisperin' and nobody listenin'
   Heard one person starve, I heard many people laughin'
   Heard the song of a poet who died in the gutter
   Heard the sound of a clown who cried in the alley
   And it's a hard, and it's a hard, it's a hard, it's a hard
   And it's a hard rain's a-gonna fall

4. Oh, who did you meet, my blue-eyed son?
   Who did you meet, my darling young one?
   I met a young child beside a dead pony
   I met a white man who walked a black dog
   I met a young woman whose body was burning
   I met a young girl, she gave me a rainbow
   I met one man who was wounded in love
   I met another man who was wounded with hatred
   And it's a hard, it's a hard, it's a hard, it's a hard
   It's a hard rain's a-gonna fall

5. Oh, what'll you do now, my blue-eyed son?
   Oh, what'll you do now, my darling young one?
   I'm a-goin' back out 'fore the rain starts a-fallin'
   I'll walk to the depths of the deepest black forest
   Where the people are many and their hands are all empty
   Where the pellets of poison are flooding their waters
   Where the home in the valley meets the damp dirty prison
   Where the executioner's face is always well hidden
   Where hunger is ugly, where souls are forgotten
   Where black is the color, where none is the number
   And I'll tell it and think it and speak it and breathe it
   And reflect it from the mountain so all souls can see it
   Then I'll stand on the ocean until I start sinkin'
   But I'll know my song well before I start singin'
   And it's a hard, it's a hard, it's a hard, it's a hard
   It's a hard rain's a-gonna fall

DON'T THINK TWICE, IT'S ALL RIGHT

The Freewheelin' Bob Dylan, 1963

This bittersweet tale of ailing romance has proved to be one of Dylan's most consistently popular songs since its appearance on *The Freewheelin' Bob Dylan*. It was recorded in November 1962, with Bruce Langhorne on guitar. Both Peter, Paul & Mary and (under the pseudonym of The Wonder Who?) The Four Seasons took the song into the US Top 20 over the next few years.

"We began admiring Bob Dylan during our visit to Paris in January [1964]. We went potty over the LP *Freewheelin'*."

John Lennon

DON'T THINK TWICE, IT'S ALL RIGHT

1. It   ain't no use _   to   sit and   won-der   why, babe _   It   don't
(2. It) ain't no use _   in   turn-in'   on   your   light, babe _   That   light

mat-ter an-y-how   An' it ain't no use _ to sit and won-der why, babe _
    I   nev-er knowed   An' it ain't no use _ in turn-in' on your light, babe _

If   you   don't   know by   now   When your roost-er   crows   at   the
I'm on the   dark side of   the   road   Still   I   wish there was   some-thin' you would

break   of   dawn   Look out your win-dow and _____   I'll   be   gone   You're   the
do   or   say   To   try and make me change my ___   mind   and   stay   We   nev-er

rea-son I'm trav-'lin'   on   Don't   think twice, it's all   right   2. It
did   too _ much talk-in' an-y - way   So don't think

right.   (3. It) ain't no use ___ in call-in' out my name, gal ___
4. I'm walk-in' down _ that long, lone-some road, babe _

Like you nev – er did be – fore   It ain't no use _ in call-in' out my
Where I'm bound, I can't _ tell   But good – bye's   too   good a

name, gal _   I   can't hear you an – y more   I'm a –
word, gal _   So I'll just say   fare thee well   I ain't

think-in' and a – won-d'rin' all the way down the road   I once loved a wom- an, _____
say – in'   you treat-ed me un – kind   You could have done   bet – ter _____

_____ a child I'm told I give her my heart but she want-ed my soul.
_____ but I don't mind You just kind-a wast-ed   my pre – cious time.

But don't think twice, It's all right   3. It   right.
But don't think twice, It's all

MASTERS OF WAR

The Freewheelin' Bob Dylan, 1963

As Dylan has insisted on many occasions, this acerbic tune was a specific attack on the military-industrial complex, although it has nevertheless become a familiar anthem of anti-war movements around the world. It was recorded during the final April 1963 session for *The Freewheelin' Bob Dylan*, a couple of months after the singer had performed it on radio for the first time.

"Bob's songs seemed to update the concepts of justice and injustice. The civil rights movement was in full bloom, and the war which would tear this nation asunder was moving towards us like a mighty storm. Before the first official bullet was fired, he had filled our arsenals with song."

Joan Baez

MASTERS OF WAR

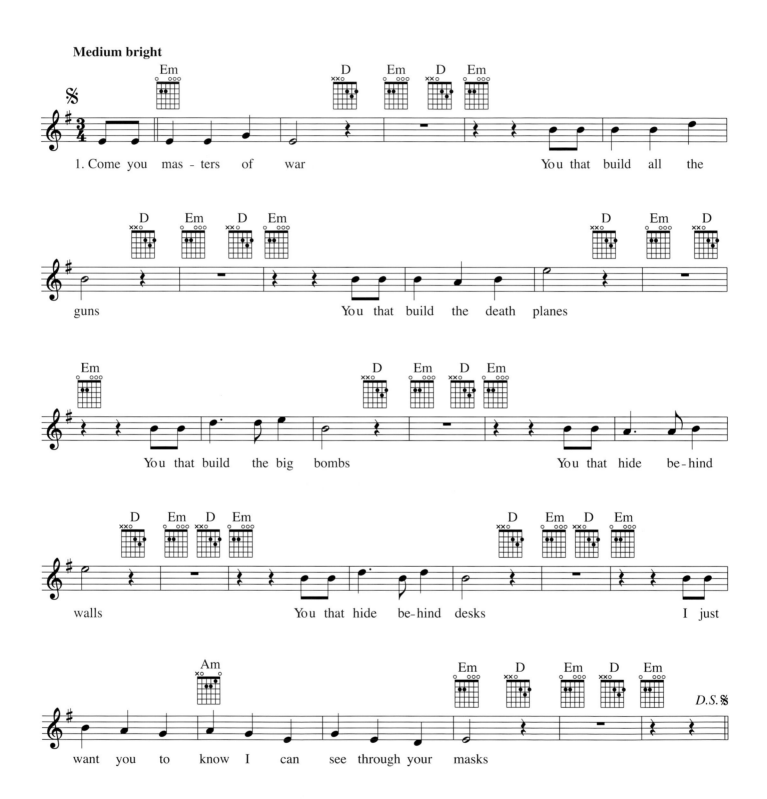

2. You that never done nothin'
   But build to destroy
   You play with my world
   Like it's your little toy
   You put a gun in my hand
   And you hide from my eyes
   And you turn and run farther
   When the fast bullets fly

3. Like Judas of old
   You lie and deceive
   A world war can be won
   You want me to believe
   But I see through your eyes
   And I see through your brain
   Like I see through the water
   That runs down my drain

4. You fasten the triggers
   For the others to fire
   Then you set back and watch
   When the death count gets higher
   You hide in your mansion
   As young people's blood
   Flows out of their bodies
   And is buried in the mud

5. You've thrown the worst fear
   That can ever be hurled
   Fear to bring children
   Into the world
   For threatening my baby
   Unborn and unnamed
   You ain't worth the blood
   That runs in your veins

6. How much do I know
   To talk out of turn
   You might say that I'm young
   You might say I'm unlearned
   But there's one thing I know
   Though I'm younger than you
   Even Jesus would never
   Forgive what you do

7. Let me ask you one question
   Is your money that good
   Will it buy you forgiveness
   Do you think that it could
   I think you will find
   When your death takes its toll
   All the money you made
   Will never buy back your soul

8. And I hope that you die
   And your death'll come soon
   I will follow your casket
   In the pale afternoon
   And I'll watch while you're lowered
   Down to your deathbed
   And I'll stand o'er your grave
   'Til I'm sure that you're dead

GIRL FROM THE NORTH COUNTRY

The Freewheelin' Bob Dylan, 1963

This nostalgic ballad, built around a traditional folk melody, was first recorded in April 1963 for *The Freewheelin' Bob Dylan.* Dylan had composed the song three months earlier during his first trip to Italy. In 1969, he revisited the song in partnership with Johnny Cash, and their duet was included as the opening track on the *Nashville Skyline* album.

GIRL FROM THE NORTH COUNTRY

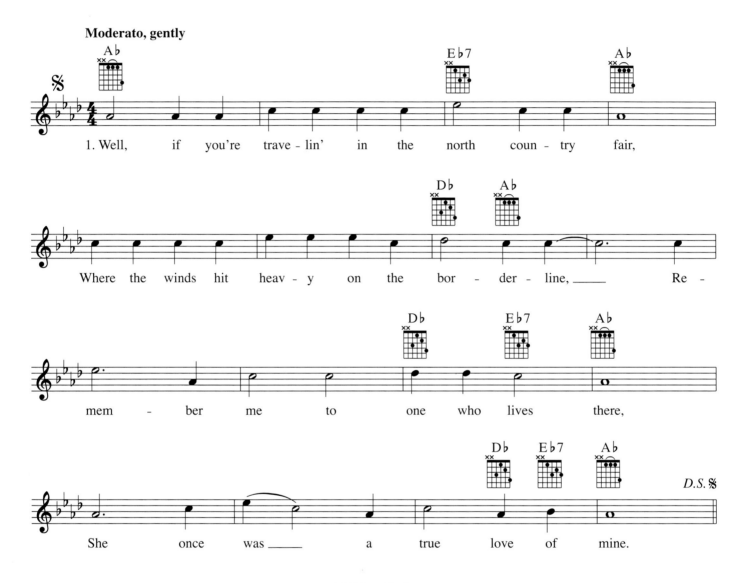

Moderato, gently

1. Well, if you're trave-lin' in the north coun-try fair,
Where the winds hit heav-y on the bor - der - line, _____ Re -
mem - ber me to one who lives there,
She once was _____ a true love of mine.

Additional lyrics

2. Well, if you go when the snowflakes storm
When the rivers freeze and summer ends
Please see if she's wearing a coat so warm
To keep her from the howlin' winds

3. Please see for me if her hair hangs long
If it rolls and flows all down her breast
Please see for me if her hair hangs long
That's the way I remember her best

4. I'm a-wonderin' if she remembers me at all
Many times I've often prayed
In the darkness of my night
In the brightness of my day

5. So if you're travelin' in the north country fair
Where the winds hit heavy on the borderline
Remember me to one who lives there
She once was a true love of mine

"To me, the person who wrote the most moving lyrics was Bob Dylan, in the early days – 'Boots Of Spanish Leather', 'Girl From The North Country'… "

Paul Simon

WITH GOD ON OUR SIDE

The Times They Are A-Changin', 1964

This song demonstrated the early sophistication of Dylan's social commentary in song. He first performed the song at New York Town Hall in April 1963, and then often performed it as a duet with Joan Baez in 1963 and 1964. His studio rendition appeared on *The Times They Are A-Changin'*, while a Dylan/Baez duet can be heard on *The Bootleg Series Vol. 6*.

"(When I heard that song) I took him seriously. I was bowled over. It was devastating. It's a very mature song. It's a beautiful song. It changed the way I thought of Bob."

Joan Baez

WITH GOD ON OUR SIDE

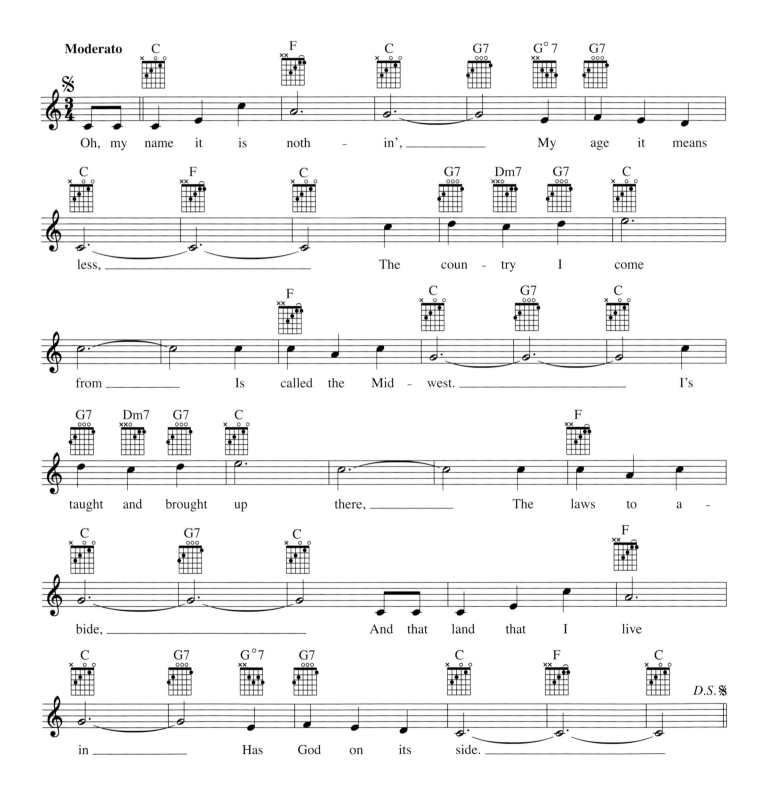

2. Oh the history books tell it
   They tell it so well
   The cavalries charged
   The Indians fell
   The cavalries charged
   The Indians died
   Oh the country was young
   With God on its side

3. Oh the Spanish-American
   War had its day
   And the Civil War too
   Was soon laid away
   And the names of the heroes
   I's made to memorize
   With guns in their hands
   And God on their side

4. Oh the First World War, boys
   It closed out its fate
   The reason for fighting
   I never got straight
   But I learned to accept it
   Accept it with pride
   For you don't count the dead
   When God's on your side

5. When the Second World War
   Came to an end
   We forgave the Germans
   And we were friends
   Though they murdered six million
   In the ovens they fried
   The Germans now too
   Have God on their side

6. I've learned to hate Russians
   All through my whole life
   If another war starts
   It's them we must fight
   To hate them and fear them
   To run and to hide
   And accept it all bravely
   With God on my side

7. But now we got weapons
   Of the chemical dust
   If fire them we're forced to
   Then fire them we must
   One push of the button
   And a shot the world wide
   And you never ask questions
   When God's on your side

8. Through many dark hour
   I've been thinkin' about this
   That Jesus Christ
   Was betrayed by a kiss
   But I can't think for you
   You'll have to decide
   Whether Judas Iscariot
   Had God on his side

9. So now as I'm leavin'
   I'm weary as Hell
   The confusion I'm feelin'
   Ain't no tongue can tell
   The words fill my head
   And fall to the floor
   If God's on our side
   He'll stop the next war

ONLY A PAWN IN THEIR GAME

The Times They Are A-Changin', 1964

Dylan responded quickly to the murder of civil rights activist Medgar Evers in June 1963. Within a few days, he had penned this sober analysis of the racist system that had spawned his killer. He debuted the song at a voter registration rally in Greenwood, Mississippi, a performance glimpsed in the *Don't Look Back* movie. He recorded it soon afterwards for *The Times They Are A-Changin'*.

"All the other protest songs were very self-righteous polemics on the terrible rednecks of the South… This song had a much more cosmic and far-reaching overview. He pointed out that the people the movement were vilifying as the enemy were really just pawns in a larger game, a game where corporate greed and the politicians were playing them against the blacks and keeping everyone down. I loved the song."

Maria Muldaur

ONLY A PAWN IN THEIR GAME

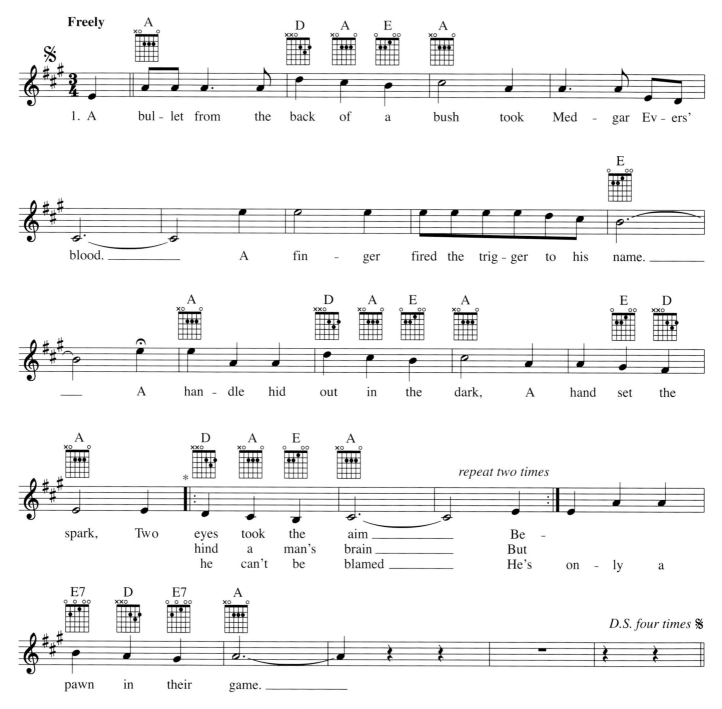

Freely

1. A bul – let from the back of a bush took Med – gar Ev – ers'

blood. _____ A fin – ger fired the trig – ger to his name. _____

_____ A han – dle hid out in the dark, A hand set the

spark, Two eyes took the aim _____ Be –
hind a man's brain _____ But
he can't be blamed _____ He's on – ly a

repeat two times

D.S. four times %

pawn in their game. _____

* Repeat as often as necessary to accommodate additional lyrics.

2. A South politician preaches to the poor white man
   "You got more than the blacks, don't complain
   You're better than them, you been born with white skin," they explain
   And the Negro's name
   Is used it is plain
   For the politician's gain
   As he rises to fame
   And the poor white remains
   On the caboose of the train
   But it ain't him to blame
   He's only a pawn in their game

3. The deputy sheriffs, the soldiers, the governors get paid
   And the marshals and cops get the same
   But the poor white man's used in the hands of them all like a tool
   He's taught in his school
   From the start by the rule
   That the laws are with him
   To protect his white skin
   To keep up his hate
   So he never thinks straight
   'Bout the shape that he's in
   But it ain't him to blame
   He's only a pawn in their game

4. From the poverty shacks, he looks from the cracks to the tracks
   And the hoofbeats pound in his brain
   And he's taught how to walk in a pack
   Shoot in the back
   With his fist in a clinch
   To hang and to lynch
   To hide 'neath the hood
   To kill with no pain
   Like a dog on a chain
   He ain't got no name
   But it ain't him to blame
   He's only a pawn in their game

5. Today, Medgar Evers was buried from the bullet he caught
   They lowered him down as a king
   But when the shadowy sun sets on the one
   That fired the gun
   He'll see by his grave
   On the stone that remains
   Carved next to his name
   His epitaph plain:
   Only a pawn in their game

THE LONESOME DEATH OF HATTIE CARROLL

The Times They Are A-Changin', 1964

This song was inspired by a callous attack on a black maid by a rich white socialite named William Zanzinger. The incident, which resulted in Hattie Carroll's death, took place in February 1963. Dylan's song was written some six months later, and appeared on his third album, *The Times They Are A-Changin'*. It continues to form a dramatic part of his live repertoire to this day.

THE LONESOME DEATH OF HATTIE CARROLL

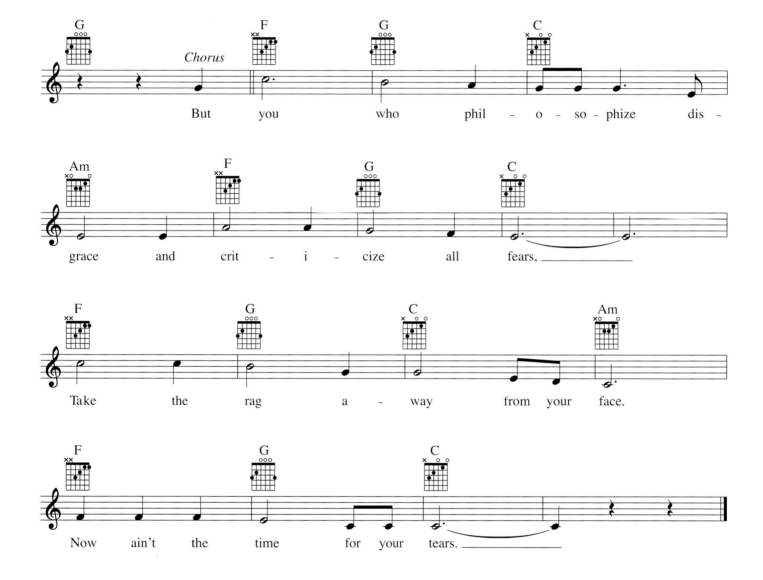

Additional lyrics

2. William Zanzinger, who at twenty-four years
   Owns a tobacco farm of six hundred acres
   With rich wealthy parents who provide and protect him
   And high office relations in the politics of Maryland
   Reacted to his deed with a shrug of his shoulders
   And swear words and sneering, and his tongue it was snarling
   In a matter of minutes on bail was out walking

   Chorus

3. Hattie Carroll was a maid of the kitchen.
   She was fifty-one years old and gave birth to ten children
   Who carried the dishes and took out the garbage
   And never sat once at the head of the table
   And didn't even talk to the people at the table
   Who just cleaned up all the food from the table
   And emptied the ashtrays on a whole other level
   Got killed by a blow, lay slain by a cane
   That sailed through the air and came down through the room
   Doomed and determined to destroy all the gentle
   And she never done nothing to William Zanzinger

   Chorus

4. In the courtroom of honor, the judge pounded his gavel
   To show that all's equal and that the courts are on the level
   And that the strings in the books ain't pulled and persuaded
   And that even the nobles get properly handled
   Once that the cops have chased after and caught 'em
   And that the ladder of law has no top and no bottom
   Stared at the person who killed for no reason
   Who just happened to be feelin' that way without warnin'
   And he spoke through his cloak, most deep and distinguished
   And handed out strongly, for penalty and repentance
   William Zanzinger with a six-month sentence

   Chorus:
   Oh, but you who philosophize disgrace and criticize all fears
   Bury the rag deep in your face
   For now's the time for your tears

"'Hattie Carroll' is a classic. It's an absolutely wonderful song, written, I'm quite sure, in a rage, but also with a great sense of form. He's a proper writer."

Martin Carthy

THE TIMES THEY ARE A-CHANGIN'

The Times They Are A-Changin', 1964

Perhaps the most famous and direct of Bob Dylan's so-called 'protest' songs, this gave its name to his third album. It was written around August 1963, and first recorded by Dylan on piano, on a demo tape for his music publisher. The more familiar guitar arrangement heard on the album was cut a few weeks later.

"Nobody could have spoken better for our generation than 'The Times They Are A-Changin''. I was already comfortable with protest songs. But with Dylan's songs it was 'Aha!'. Because they're so good. He's influenced every songwriter in rock & roll, and folk."

Joan Baez

THE TIMES THEY ARE A-CHANGIN'

2. Come writers and critics
   Who prophesize with your pen
   And keep your eyes wide
   The chance won't come again
   And don't speak too soon
   For the wheel's still in spin
   And there's no tellin' who that it's namin'
   For the loser now will be later to win
   For the times they are a-changin'

3. Come senators, congressmen
   Please heed the call
   Don't stand in the doorway
   Don't block up the hall
   For he that gets hurt
   Will be he who has stalled
   There's a battle outside and it is ragin'
   It'll soon shake your windows and rattle your walls
   For the times they are a-changin'

4. Come mothers and fathers
   Throughout the land
   And don't criticize
   What you can't understand
   Your sons and your daughters
   Are beyond your command
   Your old road is rapidly agin'
   Please get out of the new one if you can't lend your hand
   For the times they are a-changin'

5. The line it is drawn
   The curse it is cast
   The slow one now
   Will later be fast
   As the present now
   Will later be past
   The order is rapidly fadin'
   And the first one now will later be last
   For the times they are a-changin'

ONE TOO MANY MORNINGS

The Times They Are A-Changin', 1964

Originally taped in sparse acoustic form in October 1963 for Dylan's third album, *The Times They Are A-Changin'*, 'One Too Many Mornings' has resurfaced in many different guises throughout his career. Two of the most radical rearrangements are documented on record – an electric 1966 performance with The Band, on *The Bootleg Series Vol. 4*, and a rowdy Rolling Thunder Revue take from *Hard Rain* on 1976.

"'One Too Many Mornings' is a goodbye to innocence – the end of something and the beginning of something else. I love that song."

Ralph McTell

CHIMES OF FREEDOM

Another Side Of Bob Dylan, 1964

This breathtaking piece of musical poetry emerged from a road trip Dylan shared with several friends in February 1964. He debuted the song in public later that month in Berkeley, and recorded it in July for *Another Side Of Bob Dylan.* 'Chimes Of Freedom' was one of many Dylan tunes covered by The Byrds, while Bruce Springsteen and The Grateful Dead also incorporated it into their repertoires.

2. In the city's melted furnace, unexpectedly we watched
   With faces hidden while the walls were tightening
   As the echo of the wedding bells before the blowin' rain
   Dissolved into the bells of the lightning
   Tolling for the rebel, tolling for the rake
   Tolling for the luckless, the abandoned an' forsaked
   Tolling for the outcast, burnin' constantly at stake
   An' we gazed upon the chimes of freedom flashing

3. Through the mad mystic hammering of the wild ripping hail
   The sky cracked its poems in naked wonder
   That the clinging of the church bells blew far into the breeze
   Leaving only bells of lightning and its thunder
   Striking for the gentle, striking for the kind
   Striking for the guardians and protectors of the mind
   An' the unpawned painter behind beyond his rightful time
   An' we gazed upon the chimes of freedom flashing

4. Through the wild cathedral evening the rain unraveled tales
   For the disrobed faceless forms of no position
   Tolling for the tongues with no place to bring their thoughts
   All down in taken-for-granted situations
   Tolling for the deaf an' blind, tolling for the mute
   Tolling for the mistreated, mateless mother, the mistitled prostitute
   For the misdemeanor outlaw, chased an' cheated by pursuit
   An' we gazed upon the chimes of freedom flashing

5. Even though a cloud's white curtain in a far-off corner flashed
   An' the hypnotic splattered mist was slowly lifting
   Electric light still struck like arrows, fired but for the ones
   Condemned to drift or else be kept from drifting
   Tolling for the searching ones, on their speechless, seeking trail
   For the lonesome-hearted lovers with too personal a tale
   An' for each unharmful, gentle soul misplaced inside a jail
   An' we gazed upon the chimes of freedom flashing

6. Starry-eyed an' laughing as I recall when we were caught
   Trapped by no track of hours for they hanged suspended
   As we listened one last time an' we watched with one last look
   Spellbound an' swallowed 'til the tolling ended
   Tolling for the aching ones whose wounds cannot be nursed
   For the countless confused, accused, misused, strung-out ones an' worse
   An' for every hung-up person in the whole wide universe
   An' we gazed upon the chimes of freedom flashing

"Great tunes like 'Chimes Of Freedom' taught me a whole lot of what songwriting essentially is about: a three-way marriage of melody, harmonic progression and lyrics."

Bob Weir, Grateful Dead

ALL I REALLY WANT TO DO

💿 *Another Side Of Bob Dylan*, 1964

'All I Really Want To Do' was recorded alongside the rest of Dylan's fourth album, *Another Side Of Bob Dylan*, during one remarkable session on 9 June 1964. The following year, rival cover versions by The Byrds and Cher reached the UK Top 10 and the US Top 40.

"I remember playing 'All I Really Want To Do' and Bob asked, 'What was that?' I told him it was one of his songs. And he said, 'Ah ha!' He didn't recognize it."

Roger McGuinn, The Byrds

All I Really Want To Do

Moderately bright

Verse

1. I   ain't look- in' to com-
2. I   ain't look- in' to

pete   with   you,   Beat   or   cheat   or   mis - treat   you,
fight with   you,   Fright - en you   or   tight - en   you,

Sim - pli - fy   you,   clas - si - fy   you,   De - ny,   de - fy   or
Drag you down   or   drain you down,   Chain you down or

Chorus

cru - ci - fy   you.   All   I _____   real - ly _____   want to
bring you down.

(falsetto)

do _____   Is,   ba - by,   be friends with   you. _____

1.-5.   6.

2. No,   and

Additional lyrics

3. I ain't lookin' to block you up
   Shock or knock or lock you up
   Analyze you, categorize you
   Finalize you or advertise you
   All I really want to do
   Is, baby, be friends with you

4. I don't want to straight-face you
   Race or chase you, track or trace you
   Or disgrace you or displace you
   Or define you or confine you
   All I really want to do
   Is, baby, be friends with you

5. I don't want to meet your kin
   Make you spin or do you in
   Or select you or dissect you
   Or inspect you or reject you
   All I really want to do
   Is, baby, be friends with you

6. I don't want to fake you out
   Take or shake or forsake you out
   I ain't lookin' for you to feel like me
   See like me or be like me
   All I really want to do
   Is, baby, be friends with you

I DON'T BELIEVE YOU
(SHE ACTS LIKE WE NEVER HAVE MET)

Another Side Of Bob Dylan, 1964

Dylan originally recorded this song for *Another Side Of Bob Dylan* in 1964. Two years later, in a radically different electric arrangement, the song was part of his live repertoire during his final world tour for 12 years. He reprised it at The Band's Last Waltz concert in 1976, and has performed it regularly ever since.

"Bob loomed absolutely the largest. The strength and breadth of his writing during that period, it just eclipses everybody."

John Sebastian, The Lovin' Spoonful

SPANISH HARLEM INCIDENT

Another Side Of Bob Dylan, 1964

Taped during the marathon June 1964 session for *Another Side Of Bob Dylan,* 'Spanish Harlem Incident' has been performed by Bob Dylan just once since then, at New York's Philharmonic Hall that October. This performance is documented on *The Bootleg Series Vol. 6.* The Byrds added the song to their list of Dylan cover versions in 1965.

"It's hard being free in a song, getting it all in. Songs are so confining. That's why I write a lot of poetry, if that's the word."

Bob Dylan, 1964

MY BACK PAGES

 *Another Side Of Bob Dylan,* 1964

With its chorus line, 'I was so much older then, I'm younger than that now', 'My Back Pages' was widely interpreted as marking Dylan's withdrawal from social commentary when it was included on *Another Side Of Bob Dylan* in 1964. The song was included on the 1971 album *More Greatest Hits,* while a live rendition featured on the album taken from Dylan's 30th anniversary concert in 1992. Like many classic early Dylan songs, it was also covered by The Byrds.

"I don't want to write for people anymore. You know, be a spokesman. From now on, I want to write from inside me. The way I like to write is for it to come out the way I walk or talk."

Bob Dylan, 1964

IT AIN'T ME, BABE

Another Side Of Bob Dylan, 1964

Though on the surface it appears to be an ironic commentary on romance, 'It Ain't Me Babe' has taken on a richer resonance down the years in the light of its creator's relationship with his audience. It was first heard on *Another Side Of Bob Dylan* in 1964, and has consistently turned up in his live shows since then. One particularly memorable performance was captured in Dylan's panoramic film, *Renaldo & Clara.* The Turtles scored a Top 10 US hit with their cover version in 1965.

2. Go lightly from the ledge, babe
   Go lightly on the ground
   I'm not the one you want, babe
   I will only let you down
   You say you're lookin' for someone
   Who will promise never to part
   Someone to close his eyes for you
   Someone to close his heart
   Someone who will die for you an' more
   But it ain't me, babe
   No, no, no, it ain't me, babe
   It ain't me you're lookin' for, babe

3. Go melt back into the night, babe
   Everything inside is made of stone
   There's nothing in here moving
   An' anyway I'm not alone
   You say you're lookin' for someone
   Who'll pick you up each time you fall
   To gather flowers constantly
   An' to come each time you call
   A lover for your life an' nothing more
   But it ain't me, babe
   No, no, no, it ain't me, babe
   It ain't me you're lookin' for, babe

"My songs are just talking to myself. Maybe that's an egotistical thing to say, but that's what it is. I have no responsibility to anybody except myself."

Bob Dylan, 1965

TO RAMONA

Another Side Of Bob Dylan, 1964

This superb love song was originally heard on *Another Side Of Bob Dylan* in 1964, and debuted in concert shortly before the album was released. Dylan has returned to the song many times since then, rarely failing to match the quality of his original performance. Despite its very personal nature, 'To Ramona' was covered by The Flying Burrito Brothers in 1971.

"That was just somebody I knew. I think I'd played this for the first time at the Gaslight, probably after hours."

Bob Dylan, 1985

SUBTERRANEAN HOMESICK BLUES

Bringing It All Back Home, 1965

As the first track on 1965's *Bringing It All Back Home* album, 'Subterranean Homesick Blues' shocked many of Dylan's more conservative admirers with its rock 'n' roll rhythms and electric accompaniment. It has passed into history as the subject of the first 'video', shot outside a London hotel in May 1965. The song provided an appropriate opening salvo to the first concert of Dylan's so-called 'never-ending' tour, in June 1988.

"It's from Chuck Berry, a bit of 'Too Much Monkey Business', and some of the scat songs of the 1940s."

Bob Dylan, 2004

MAGGIE'S FARM

🎵 *Bringing It All Back Home,* 1965

This hilarious commentary on hypocrisy and greed, first exposed to the world on *Bringing It All Back Home* in 1965, became an all-purpose anthem in subsequent decades. British radicals adopted it as their own during the leadership of Margaret 'Maggie' Thatcher in the 1980s. The song has been a staple part of Dylan's live repertoire for more than 40 years, and a particularly edgy interpretation provided the opening track for the *Hard Rain* album in 1976.

"This was electricity married to content. We were hearing music with lyrics that had a meaning, with a rock beat, drums and electric guitars. Absolutely stunning."

Jac Holzman, founder of Elektra Records

MR. TAMBOURINE MAN

Bringing It All Back Home, 1965

Alongside 'Blowin' In The Wind', 'Mr Tambourine Man' is perhaps Bob Dylan's most famous song – thanks in part to the global success of The Byrds' folk-rock version in 1965. He began to write it in February 1964, and debuted it a few weeks later during a concert in London. Dylan built his complex web of imagery around a central figure inspired by his friend and session guitarist Bruce Langhorne.

"On one session, [producer] Tom Wilson had asked Bruce to play tambourine. And he had this gigantic tambourine, it was as big as a wagon-wheel. He was playing, and this vision of him playing this tambourine just stuck in my mind."

Bob Dylan, 1985

2. Take me on a trip upon your magic swirlin' ship
   My senses have been stripped, my hands can't feel to grip
   My toes too numb to step
   Wait only for my boot heels to be wanderin'
   I'm ready to go anywhere, I'm ready for to fade
   Into my own parade, cast your dancing spell my way
   I promise to go under it

Refrain

3. Though you might hear laughin', spinnin', swingin' madly across the sun
   It's not aimed at anyone, it's just escapin' on the run
   And but for the sky there are no fences facin'
   And if you hear vague traces of skippin' reels of rhyme
   To your tambourine in time, it's just a ragged clown behind
   I wouldn't pay it any mind
   It's just a shadow you're seein' that he's chasin'

Refrain

4. Then take me disappearin' through the smoke rings of my mind
   Down the foggy ruins of time, far past the frozen leaves
   The haunted, frightened trees, out to the windy beach
   Far from the twisted reach of crazy sorrow
   Yes, to dance beneath the diamond sky with one hand waving free
   Silhouetted by the sea, circled by the circus sands
   With all memory and fate driven deep beneath the waves
   Let me forget about today until tomorrow

Refrain

"When I heard him sing that song, I started crying. I knew I was seeing the emergence of a major artist."

Liam Clancy

IT'S ALRIGHT, MA (I'M ONLY BLEEDING)

Bringing It All Back Home, 1965

The audience at New York's Philharmonic Hall in October 1964 was the first to hear this stunning lyrical extravaganza, set to a fierce acoustic blues riff. Three months later, Dylan recorded the song for *Bringing It All Back Home*. He has performed the song countless times since then, rekindling its blues roots with his thrilling electric arrangements in recent years.

"I've written some songs that I look at, and they just give me a sense of awe. Stuff like 'It's Alright Ma', just the alliteration in that blows me away."

Bob Dylan, 1997

2. As some warn victory, some downfall
   Private reasons great or small
   Can be seen in the eyes of those that call
   To make all that should be killed to crawl
   While others say don't hate nothing at all
   Except hatred

   Disillusioned words like bullets bark
   As human gods aim for their mark
   Made everything from toy guns that spark
   To flesh-colored Christs that glow in the dark
   It's easy to see without looking too far
   That not much is really sacred

   While preachers preach of evil fates
   Teachers teach that knowledge waits
   Can lead to hundred-dollar plates
   Goodness hides behind its gates
   But even the president of the United States
   Sometimes must have to stand naked

   An' though the rules of the road have been lodged
   It's only people's games that you got to dodge
   And it's alright, Ma, I can make it

3. Advertising signs that con
   You into thinking you're the one
   That can do what's never been done
   That can win what's never been won
   Meantime life outside goes on
   All around you

   You lose yourself, you reappear
   You suddenly find you got nothing to fear
   Alone you stand with nobody near
   When a trembling distant voice, unclear
   Startles your sleeping ears to hear
   That somebody thinks they really found you

   A question in your nerves is lit
   Yet you know there is no answer fit
   To satisfy insure you not to quit
   To keep it in your mind and not forget
   That it is not he or she or them or it
   That you belong to

   Although the masters make the rules
   For the wise men and the fools
   I got nothing, Ma, to live up to

4. For them that must obey authority
   That they do not respect in any degree
   Who despise their jobs, their destinies
   Speak jealously of them that are free
   Cultivate their flowers to be
   Nothing more than something they invest in

   While some on principles baptized
   To strict party platform ties
   Social clubs in drag disguise
   Outsiders they can freely criticize
   Tell nothing except who to idolize
   And then say God bless him

   While one who sings with his tongue on fire
   Gargles in the rat race choir
   Bent out of shape from society's pliers
   Cares not to come up any higher
   But rather get you down in the hole
   That he's in

   But I mean no harm nor put fault
   On anyone that lives in a vault
   But it's alright, Ma, if I can't please him

5. Old lady judges watch people in pairs
   Limited in sex, they dare
   To push fake morals, insult and stare
   While money doesn't talk, it swears
   Obscenity, who really cares
   Propaganda, all is phony

   While them that defend what they cannot see
   With a killer's pride, security
   It blows the minds most bitterly
   For them that think death's honesty
   Won't fall upon them naturally
   Life sometimes must get lonely

   My eyes collide head-on with stuffed
   Graveyards false gods, I scuff
   At pettiness which plays so rough
   Walk upside-down inside handcuffs
   Kick my legs to crash it off
   Say okay, I have had enough what else can you show me?

   And if my thought-dreams could be seen
   They'd probably put my head in a guillotine
   But it's alright, Ma, it's life, and life only

"He has, at certain moments in his writing career, crystallized stuff so well that it will last for a thousand years of human history. If we don't destroy ourselves by then, in the year 3000 someone somewhere will be singing, 'He not busy being born is busy dying'. That's significant. That's really making a contribution to your art."

David Crosby

GATES OF EDEN

🎵 *Bringing It All Back Home*, 1965

This song was taped at the same January 1965 session as 'Mr Tambourine Man' and 'It's All Right, Ma (I'm Only Bleeding)' for the *Bringing It All Back Home* album. Its debut live performance, taped at New York's Philharmonic Hall on Halloween night 1964, was released on *The Bootleg Series Vol. 6*.

"It is an amazing song. So many of the songs he wrote around that time were influenced by people like Martin Carthy, and by his trips over to England and his absorption of traditional forms. It is not a giant step from what Bob played on 'Gates Of Eden' to an Irish or Scottish tune."

Ralph McTell

LOVE MINUS ZERO/NO LIMIT

Bringing It All Back Home, 1965

Lyrical and hypnotic, 'Love Minus Zero/No Limit' has proved to be one of the most enduring songs from Dylan's 1965 masterpiece, *Bringing It All Back Home.* The studio recording was made that January, and Dylan swiftly added the song to his live sets that spring. The Turtles and Joan Baez are among the other artists to have tackled the song on record.

"Songwriting is like fishing in a stream: you put in your line and hope you catch something. And I don't think anyone downstream from Bob Dylan ever caught anything."

Arlo Guthrie

SHE BELONGS TO ME

Bringing It All Back Home, 1965

Few albums in history have produced as many 'standard' songs as *Bringing It All Back Home*. 'She Belongs To Me' is merely one of half-a-dozen Dylan compositions recorded in January 1965 that have become indelibly associated with his name, and regularly appeared in his live set-lists. Much covered in the 1960s, it was recorded by acts as diverse as country-rocker Rick Nelson and prog-rockers The Nice.

"I love that song, it's beautiful. I really think that you can hear his Buddy Holly influence coming out on that one."

Donovan

IT'S ALL OVER NOW, BABY BLUE

🎵 *Bringing It All Back Home*, 1965

This elegiac song completed both Dylan's groundbreaking 1965 album *Bringing It All Back Home* and his controversial appearance at that summer's Newport Folk Festival. One of his most covered tunes, it has been recorded by such notable artists as The Grateful Dead, Them (with Van Morrison), Joan Baez, The Byrds, Leon Russell and The Animals.

"I had carried that song around in my head for a long time, and I remember that when I was writing it, I'd remembered a Gene Vincent song, 'Baby Blue'. It had always been one of my favourites."

Bob Dylan, 1985

BOB DYLAN'S 115TH DREAM

Bringing It All Back Home, 1965

This song featured at the end of the 'electric' side of Dylan's 1965 album, *Bringing It All Back Home* – complete with a false start that harked back to a similar moment on a ten-year-old Elvis Presley single. Dylan was supported by a small group featuring Bill Lee, John Hammond Jr., Bobby Gregg and guitar genius Bruce Langhorne.

10. Well, I got back and took
The parkin' ticket off the mast
I was ripping it to shreds
When this coastguard boat went past
They asked me my name
And I said, "Captain Kidd"
They believed me but
They wanted to know
What exactly that I did
I said for the Pope of Eruke
I was employed
They let me go right away
They were very paranoid

11. Well, the last I heard of Arab
He was stuck on a whale
That was married to the deputy
Sheriff of the jail
But the funniest thing was
When I was leavin' the bay
I saw three ships a-sailin'
They were all heading my way
I asked the captain what his name was
And how come he didn't drive a truck
He said his name was Columbus
I just said, "Good luck"

"We didn't know where to cut the groove. So he went, 'I was ridin' on the Mayflower…', and we all should have come in on 'ridin', but everyone sat there."

Bruce Langhorne

LIKE A ROLLING STONE

🄿 *Highway 61 Revisited,* 1965

Arguably the most important rock song of all time, 'Like A Rolling Stone' altered the landscape of popular music when it was released as a single in 1965. It subsequently became the opening track on *Highway 61 Revisited.* Since then, it has rarely left Dylan's live repertoire, and it remains as stirring and anthemic today as it was more than 40 years ago.

"When I heard 'Like A Rolling Stone', I wanted to quit the music business."

Frank Zappa

Additional lyrics

2. You've gone to the finest school all right, Miss Lonely
   But you know you only used to get juiced in it
   And nobody has ever taught you how to live on the street
   And now you find out you're gonna have to get used to it
   You said you'd never compromise
   With the mystery tramp, but now you realize
   He's not selling any alibis
   As you stare into the vacuum of his eyes
   And ask him do you want to make a deal?

Refrain

3. You never turned around to see the frowns on the jugglers and the clowns
   When they all come down and did tricks for you
   You never understood that it ain't no good
   You shouldn't let other people get your kicks for you
   You used to ride on the chrome horse with your diplomat
   Who carried on his shoulder a Siamese cat
   Ain't it hard when you discover that
   He really wasn't where it's at
   After he took from you everything he could steal

Refrain

4. Princess on the steeple and all the pretty people
   They're drinkin', thinkin' that they got it made
   Exchanging all kinds of precious gifts and things
   But you'd better lift your diamond ring, you'd better pawn it babe
   You used to be so amused
   At Napoleon in rags and the language that he used
   Go to him now, he calls you, you can't refuse
   When you got nothing, you got nothing to lose
   You're invisible now, you got no secrets to conceal

Refrain

"The first time I heard Bob Dylan, I was in the car with my mother, listening to WMCA, and on came that snare shot that sounded like somebody'd kicked open the door to your mind – 'Like A Rolling Stone'. I knew that I was listening to the toughest voice that I had ever heard. It was lean and it sounded somehow simultaneously young and adult."

Bruce Springsteen

TOMBSTONE BLUES

🎧 *Highway 61 Revisited*, 1965

The second track on the landmark *Highway 61 Revisited* album, 'Tombstone Blues' was recorded in July 1965. The released mix was a propulsive slice of urban blues, illuminated by Michael Bloomfield's quicksilver guitar fills. A different version, heard on *The Bootleg Series Vol. 7*, featured vocal support from the R&B group, the Chambers Brothers. The song's first public performance followed a month later, at Forest Hills stadium in New York.

Additional lyrics

2. The hysterical bride in the penny arcade
   Screaming she moans, "I've just been made"
   Then sends out for the doctor who pulls down the shade
   Says, "My advice is to not let the boys in"

3. Now the medicine man comes and he shuffles inside
   He walks with a swagger and he says to the bride
   "Stop all this weeping, swallow your pride
   You will not die, it's not poison"

   Chorus

4. Well, John the Baptist after torturing a thief
   Looks up at his hero the Commander-in-Chief
   Saying, "Tell me great hero, but please make it brief
   Is there a hole for me to get sick in?"

5. The Commander-in-Chief answers him while chasing a fly
   Saying, "Death to all those who would whimper and cry"
   And dropping a bar bell he points to the sky
   Saying, "The sun's not yellow it's chicken"

   Chorus

6. The king of the Philistines his soldiers to save
   Puts jawbones on their tombstones and flatters their graves
   Puts the pied pipers in prison and fattens the slaves
   Then sends them out to the jungle

7. Gypsy Davey with a blowtorch he burns out their camps
   With his faithful slave Pedro behind him he tramps
   With a fantastic collection of stamps
   To win friends and influence his uncle

   Chorus

8. The geometry of innocence flesh on the bone
   Causes Galileo's math book to get thrown
   At Delilah who sits worthlessly alone
   But the tears on her cheeks are from laughter

9. Now I wish I could give Brother Bill his great thrill
   I would set him in chains at the top of the hill
   Then send out for some pillars and Cecil B. DeMille
   He could die happily ever after

   Chorus

10. Where Ma Raney and Beethoven once unwrapped their bed roll
    Tuba players now rehearse around the flagpole
    And the National Bank at a profit sells road maps for the soul
    To the old folks home and the college

11. Now I wish I could write you a melody so plain
    That could hold you dear lady from going insane
    That could ease you and cool you and cease the pain
    Of your useless and pointless knowledge

    Chorus

"Dylan's Woody Guthrie period was very nice and I liked him then, but he had a second wave of popularity when he became more psychedelic… and at that time John [Lennon] particularly became very enamoured of him because of his poetry. All those songs were great lyrically."

Paul McCartney

IT TAKES A LOT TO LAUGH, IT TAKES A TRAIN TO CRY

🎵 *Highway 61 Revisited, 1965*

This blues-inflected song began life in a rousing electric arrangement, before Dylan hit upon the more reflective version heard on 1965's *Highway 61 Revisited*. One of his most memorable live renditions was heard at George Harrison's Concert For Bangladesh in August 1971. Al Kooper, who performed on Dylan's original recording with Michael Bloomfield, revisited the song on his million-selling *Super Session* album.

IT TAKES A LOT TO LAUGH,
IT TAKES A TRAIN TO CRY

Medium slow blues tempo

1. Well, I ride on a mail train, babe, __ Can't buy a thrill. __

Well, I've been up all night, __ baby Lean-in' on the win-dow sill. __

Well, if I die __ on top of the hill _____ And

if I don't make it ____ You know my ba-by will. __

repeat two times

Additional lyrics

2. Don't the moon look good, mama
   Shinin' through the trees?
   Don't the brakeman look good, mama
   Flagging down the "Double E?"
   Don't the sun look good
   Goin' down over the sea?
   Don't my gal look fine
   When she's comin' after me?

3. Now the wintertime is coming
   The windows are filled with frost
   I went to tell everybody
   But I could not get across
   Well, I wanna be your lover, baby
   I don't wanna be your boss
   Don't say I never warned you
   When your train gets lost

"Bob is a weird cat, you know: weird music, weird words, weird session. But I liked the songs. He sings them, and the musicians fit themselves around them. He sings these long, complex meaningful songs. He's a poet."

Michael Bloomfield

HIGHWAY 61 REVISITED

Highway 61 Revisited, 1965

The title song of Bob Dylan's classic 1965 album featured Michael Bloomfield on lead guitar and Dylan himself adding a police siren. More than 40 years later, 'Highway 61 Revisited' remains a staple part of his live shows. Terry Reid and Johnny Winter are among the few artists who have been brave enough to cover this Dylan anthem.

"From the moment I met him I thought he was great, a genius, Shakespearean. Every succeeding album up to *Highway 61*, I had an increasing lot of secret fear: 'Oh my God, what can he do next? He can't possibly top that one.' And then I put on *Highway 61*, and I laughed and said it's so ridiculous. It's impossibly good, it just can't be that good. How can a human mind do this?"

Phil Ochs

BALLAD OF A THIN MAN

Highway 61 Revisited, 1965

This enigmatic song about the incomprehension of 'Mr Jones' has been a regular feature of Dylan's live shows since its first appearance on the *Highway 61 Revisited* album in 1965. Dylan himself played the distinctive piano part, supported by a stellar band including guitar legend Michael Bloomfield, and Al Kooper on organ.

2. You raise up your head
   And you ask, "Is this where it is?"
   And somebody points to you and says
   "It's his"
   And you say, "What's mine?"
   And somebody else says, "Where what is?"
   And you say, "Oh my God
   Am I here all alone?"

   Because something is happening here
   But you don't know what it is
   Do you, Mister Jones?

3. You hand in your ticket
   And you go watch the geek
   Who immediately walks up to you
   When he hears you speak
   And says, "How does it feel
   To be such a freak?"
   And you say, "Impossible"
   As he hands you a bone

   Because something is happening here
   But you don't know what it is
   Do you, Mister Jones?

   Bridge:
   You have many contacts
   Among the lumberjacks
   To get you facts
   When someone attacks your imagination
   But nobody has any respect
   Anyway they already expect you
   To just give a check
   To tax-deductible charity organizations

4. You've been with the professors
   And they've all liked your looks
   With great lawyers you have
   Discussed lepers and crooks
   You've been through all of
   F. Scott Fitzgerald's books
   You're very well read
   It's well known

   Because something is happening here
   But you don't know what it is
   Do you, Mister Jones?

5. Well, the sword swallower, he comes up to you
   And then he kneels
   He crosses himself
   And then he clicks his high heels
   And without further notice
   He asks you how it feels
   And he says, "Here is your throat back
   Thanks for the loan"

   Because something is happening here
   But you don't know what it is
   Do you, Mister Jones?

6. Now you see this one-eyed midget
   Shouting the word "NOW"
   And you say, "For what reason?"
   And he says, "How?"
   And you say, "What does this mean?"
   And he screams back, "You're a cow
   Give me some milk
   Or else go home"

   Because something is happening here
   But you don't know what it is
   Do you, Mister Jones?

7. Well, you walk into the room
   Like a camel and then you frown
   You put your eyes in your pocket
   And your nose on the ground
   There ought to be a law
   Against you comin' around
   You should be made
   To wear earphones

   Because something is happening here
   But you don't know what it is
   Do you, Mister Jones?

"It tells that person who's lame that they're lame, and why they're lame, which is a very satisfying thing to do. Being able to do that and do it beautifully – to me, that's wonderful. That's something that only Dylan has been able to pull off in terms of modern songwriting, I think."

Jerry Garcia, Grateful Dead

QUEEN JANE APPROXIMATELY

Highway 61 Revisited, 1965

Rich and evocative, 'Queen Jane Approximately' opened the second side of 1965's *Highway 61 Revisited* album. Rumours that he performed the song live that year have never been confirmed, so its first known public performance came 22 years later, on Independence Day in 1987, with The Grateful Dead. A later rendition from that tour was subsequently included on the *Dylan & The Dead* CD.

"Dylan gave rock 'n' roll the thing I'd wished it had when I was a kid – respectability, some authority. He took it out of the realm of ignorant guys banging away on electric instruments and put it somewhere else altogether."

Jerry Garcia, Grateful Dead

DESOLATION ROW

⊙ *Highway 61 Revisited*, 1965

As the closing track of his landmark 1965 album *Highway 61 Revisited*, Dylan unveiled this epic, 11-minute song, on which guitarist Michael Bloomfield contributed some of his most lyrical playing. 'Desolation Row' immediately became a cornerstone of Dylan's live shows, and it has remained in his repertoire to this day.

"I do know what my songs are about. Some are about four minutes, some are about five, and some, believe it or not, are about 11 or 12."

Bob Dylan, 1966

POSITIVELY 4TH STREET

Bob Dylan's Greatest Hits, 1967

A non-album hit single from 1965, 'Positively 4th Street' was perhaps the most outspoken and direct 'pop' song ever written up to that point. Dylan never explained who the song was aimed at, but the ferocity and contempt of its lyrics remains undimmed after more than four decades.

"That particular song showed me – I remember thinking, 'The American pop song has finally grown up. You can sing about anything now.' When he sang, 'You got a lot of nerve to say you are my friend', just in that statement was a different song than any I had ever heard."

Joni Mitchell

POSITIVELY 4TH STREET

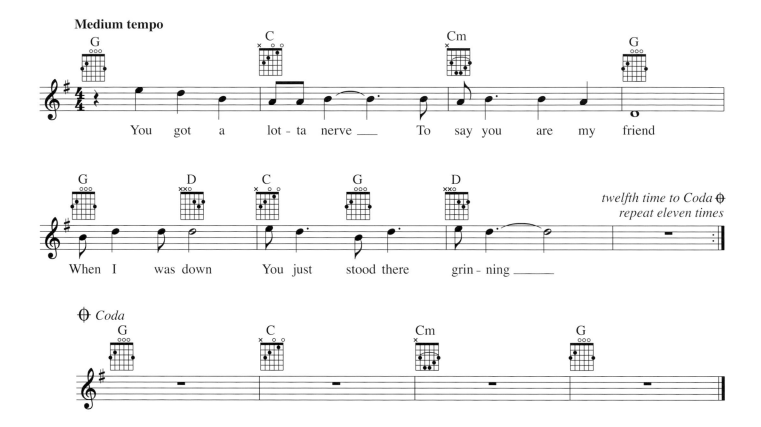

Medium tempo

G   C   Cm   G

You got a lot-ta nerve ___ To say you are my friend

G   D   C   G   D

twelfth time to Coda
repeat eleven times

When I was down You just stood there grin - ning ___

Coda

G   C   Cm   G

2. You got a lotta nerve
   To say you got a helping hand to lend
   You just want to be on
   The side that's winning

3. You say I let you down
   You know it's not like that
   If you're so hurt
   Why then don't you show it

4. You say you lost your faith
   But that's not where it's at
   You had no faith to lose
   And you know it

5. I know the reason
   That you talk behind my back
   I used to be among the crowd
   You're in with

6. Do you take me for such a fool
   To think I'd make contact
   With the one who tries to hide
   What he don't know to begin with

7. You see me on the street
   You always act surprised
   You say, "How are you?" "Good luck"
   But you don't mean it

8. When you know as well as me
   You'd rather see me paralyzed
   Why don't you just come out once
   And scream it

9. No, I do not feel that good
   When I see the heartbreaks you embrace
   If I was a master thief
   Perhaps I'd rob them

10. And now I know you're dissatisfied
    With your position and your place
    Don't you understand
    It's not my problem

11. I wish that for just one time
    You could stand inside my shoes
    And just for that one moment
    I could be you

12. Yes, I wish that for just one time
    You could stand inside my shoes
    You'd know what a drag it is
    To see you

VISIONS OF JOHANNA

💿 *Blonde On Blonde, 1966*

Often described as Dylan's greatest song, 'Visions Of Johanna' was written in late 1965 (under the provisional title of 'Freeze Out'), and recorded on two occasions with the future members of The Band before the take captured for posterity on *Blonde On Blonde* was achieved in Nashville. Dylan was already performing the song before the album was released, and its occasional appearances in his set-lists are eagerly awaited to this day.

"'Mona Lisa must have had the highway blues' – it's just a great observation. He's commenting on it in a way that nobody had done, and yet was very contemporary. He came out of that tradition of Woody Guthrie and Jack Kerouac – the road, hitch-hiking, that long line of male guitar-slingers hitch-hiking with guitars over their back, and that was related to the hobo tradition. You knew what the 'highway blues' were, but your parents didn't!"

Loudon Wainwright III

VISIONS OF JOHANNA

Moderately slow

1. Ain't it   just like the night __ to play   tricks when you're try-in' to be so
   lot   where the la - dies play   blind - man's bluff   with the
   lit - tle boy   lost, __   he   takes him-self   so   se - ri - ous
   side   the mu - se - ums,   In - fin - i - ty   goes   up on

qui - et? _____   We   sit here   strand - ed,   though we're all __
key chain _____   And the   all - night   girls   they whis-
ly _____   He   brags of   his   mis - er - y,   he likes_
tri - al _____   Voic - es   ech - o   this is   what   sal -

do - in' our best   to   de - ny ___   it _____   And Lou-
per of es - ca-pades out   on the "D" ___   train _____   We can
to live   dan - ger-our-ly ___   And when
va - tion must   be   like af - ter a   while _   But Mo - na

ise   holds a   hand-ful of rain,   tempt - in' you _   to   de -
hear   the night watch - man click his flash-light   Ask him-self if it's him or them that's real-ly in -
bring - ing her name up   He speaks of a   fare - well kiss _   to
Li - sa must-a   had   the high - way blues   You can tell __   by the way   she

fy it _____
sane _____
me _____
smiles _____

Lights   flick- er   from _ the op - po - site
Lou - ise,   she's all right, she's just
He's   sure   got _ a   lot - ta
See the prim- i - tive _ wall - flow- er

loft   In   this   room   the heat pipes   just cough   The
near   She's del - i - cate   and seems like   the   mir - ror _____   But she just
gall   to   be   so   use - less   and   all   Mut - ter -
freeze   When the jel - ly -   faced wom- en   all   sneeze   Hear the

coun - try mu - sic sta - tion plays soft   But there's noth-ing, real- ly noth- ing   to   turn
makes it   all __ too con- cise and too clear   That Jo - han- na's   not here
ing   small talk _ at   the wall   while I'm   in the
one   with_ the mus- tache   say, "Jeeze, I   can't   find my knees."

off

Just   Lou - ise   and her
The   ghost   of 'lec - tric- i - ty

hall   How   can   I   ex - plain?   Oh,
                    Oh,   jewels   and bin - oc - u - lars

lov - er   so   en - twined _____   And   these vi- sions_
howls   in   the bones   of   her   face _____   Where these vi- sions_
it's   so   hard   to   get   on _____   And   these vi- sions_
hang   from the head   of   the   mule _____   But   these vi- sions_

179

I WANT YOU

Blonde On Blonde, 1966

'I Want You' was a Top 20 hit single on both sides of the Atlantic in 1966, when it was one of the highlights of Dylan's double album, *Blonde On Blonde*. Although it didn't feature in his live sets that year, it did later appear on two of his concert albums, *Bob Dylan At Budokan* and *Dylan & The Dead*.

JUST LIKE A WOMAN

Blonde On Blonde, 1966

This touching, troubling commentary on sexual relations was recorded for *Blonde On Blonde* in March 1966. Dylan's single reached the US Top 40 that year, while in Britain Manfred Mann's cover version stole the chart action. Often performed by Dylan in concert, the song provided a memorable climax to his brief set at the Concert For Bangladesh in 1971.

"'Just Like A Woman' is a hard song to pin down. It's one of those that you can sing a thousand times and still ask, 'what is it about?', but you know there's a real feeling there."

Bob Dylan, 1992

STUCK INSIDE OF MOBILE
WITH THE MEMPHIS BLUES AGAIN

Blonde On Blonde, 1966

It may have taken almost 18 hours to perfect in the studio, but 'Stuck Inside Of Mobile' epitomised the "wild mercury sound" that Dylan proudly recalled as the trademark of his 1966 double album, *Blonde On Blonde*. Ten years later, Dylan performed the song publicly for the first time with the Rolling Thunder Revue, and a rendition from Fort Worth was included on his *Hard Rain* album.

6. Now the preacher looked so baffled
   When I asked him why he dressed
   With twenty pounds of headlines
   Stapled to his chest
   But he cursed me when I proved it to him
   Then I whispered, "Not even you can hide
   You see, you're just like me
   I hope you're satisfied"

   Chorus

7. Now the rainman gave me two cures
   Then he said, "Jump right in"
   The one was Texas medicine
   The other was just railroad gin
   An' like a fool I mixed them
   An' it strangled up my mind
   An' now people just get uglier
   An' I have no sense of time

   Chorus

8. When Ruthie says come see her
   In her honky-tonk lagoon
   Where I can watch her waltz for free
   'Neath her Panamanian moon
   An' I say, "Aw come on now
   You must know about my debutante"
   An' she says, "Your debutante just knows what you need
   But I know what you want"

   Chorus

9. Now the bricks lay on Grand Street
   Where the neon madmen climb
   They all fall there so perfectly
   It all seems so well timed
   An' here I sit so patiently
   Waiting to find out what price
   You have to pay to get out of
   Going through all these things twice

   Chorus

"That record's unbelievable. It's triumphant and defiant and thrilling from beginning to end. The drums, man. It's Kenny Buttrey. I actually get choked up sometimes listening to those snare fills. I can't believe how beautiful it is."

Frank Black, The Pixies

MOST LIKELY YOU GO YOUR WAY
(AND I'LL GO MINE)

Blonde On Blonde, 1966

Like most of the *Blonde On Blonde* album, this song was recorded at Columbia's Nashville studios in the early weeks of 1966. Amongst the musicians who took part in the sessions were future rock stars Al Kooper and Joe South, alongside Robbie Robertson (soon to become the leader of The Band). At many of the shows on Dylan's 1974 US tour with The Band, he used this song both to open and close his sets.

"I was the janitor in the studio during the *Blonde On Blonde* sessions. I wouldn't have dared interrupt his creation, but I was captivated. To me, he was the measuring stick – the standard – by which everyone else was measured. Like Muhammad Ali!"

Kris Kristofferson

SAD-EYED LADY OF THE LOWLANDS

Blonde On Blonde, 1966

The release of this song on *Blonde On Blonde* marked the first occasion in rock history that a single track had been allowed to fill an entire side of an album. It was written while the musicians were waiting in the studio for the session to begin, and as they began to record, none of them realised that the song was about to last for more than 12 minutes.

2. With your sheets like metal and your belt like lace
   And your deck of cards missing the jack and the ace
   And your basement clothes and your hollow face
   Who among them can think he could outguess you?
   With your silhouette when the sunlight dims
   Into your eyes where the moonlight swims
   And your matchbook songs and your gypsy hymns
   Who among them would try to impress you?

   Chorus

3. The kings of Tyrus with their convict list
   Are waiting in line for their geranium kiss
   And you wouldn't know it would happen like this
   But who among them really wants just to kiss you?
   With your childhood flames on your midnight rug
   And your Spanish manners and your mother's drugs
   And your cowboy mouth and your curfew plugs
   Who among them do you think could resist you?

   Chorus

4. Oh, the farmers and the businessmen, they all did decide
   To show you the dead angels that they used to hide
   But why did they pick you to sympathize with their side?
   Oh, how could they ever mistake you?
   They wished you'd accepted the blame for the farm
   But with the sea at your feet and the phony false alarm
   And with the child of a hoodlum wrapped up in your arms
   How could they ever, ever persuade you?

   Chorus

5. With your sheet-metal memory of Cannery Row
   And your magazine-husband who one day just had to go
   And your gentleness now, which you just can't help but show
   Who among them do you think would employ you?
   Now you stand with your thief, you're on his parole
   With your holy medallion which your fingertips fold
   And your saintlike face and your ghostlike soul
   Oh, who among them do you think could destroy you

   Chorus

"It was a first take. Not knowing how long this thing was going to be, we were preparing ourselves for a basic two-to-three-minute record. After about ten minutes of this thing, we were cracking up at each other. I mean, we peaked five minutes ago! Where do we go from here?"

Kenny Buttrey, drummer on *Blonde On Blonde*

I SHALL BE RELEASED

Bob Dylan's Greatest Hits, Vol. 2, 1971

When the so-called 'Basement Tapes' began to circulate amongst musicians and fans in the late 1960s, 'I Shall Be Released' registered as an instant Dylan standard. It was covered by his former backing group, The Band, on their *Music From Big Pink* album. Dylan re-recorded the song in 1971 for his *More Greatest Hits* album, and has performed it in a dazzling variety of arrangements ever since. 'I Shall Be Released' has also acted as a closing anthem for many all-star benefits down the years.

"He was writing shorter lines, with every line meaning something. Each line had to advance the story, bring the song forward… There was to be no wasted language, no wasted breath… And from that came some of the stuff that he did with The Band, like 'I Shall Be Released'."

Allen Ginsberg

QUINN THE ESKIMO (THE MIGHTY QUINN)

💿 *Self Portrait*, 1970

The British pop group Manfred Mann first brought this song to public attention, when their cover version (titled 'The Mighty Quinn') topped the UK charts in early 1968. They had been sent a tape of Bob Dylan's original 'Basement Tapes' recording, made with the future members of The Band the previous year. In 1969, Dylan and The Band played 'Quinn The Eskimo' at the Isle of Wight festival, and this performance was included on Dylan's 1970 release *Self Portrait*.

"I think Dylan really loved the stuff we did, and in the 60s he said he preferred our versions to anyone else's. That's because we treated them with a lack of respect and changed things around, rather than just copying him."

Manfred Mann

YOU AIN'T GOIN' NOWHERE

🎧 *Bob Dylan's Greatest Hits, Vol. 2, 1971*

One of the legendary 'Basement Tapes' songs, 'You Ain't Goin' Nowhere' was committed to tape with two very different sets of lyrics. The more conventional of them was covered by The Byrds in 1968, ensuring that the song became a country-rock standard. Dylan returned to the song in 1971, for his *More Greatest Hits* album, but didn't debut it on the road until 1997.

"We were one of the first people to hear his basement tape. That song just jumped out at us. It seemed to fit in perfectly with what we wanted to do when we were cutting that country album *Sweetheart Of The Rodeo* down in Nashville."

Chris Hillman, The Byrds

YOU AIN'T GOIN' NOWHERE

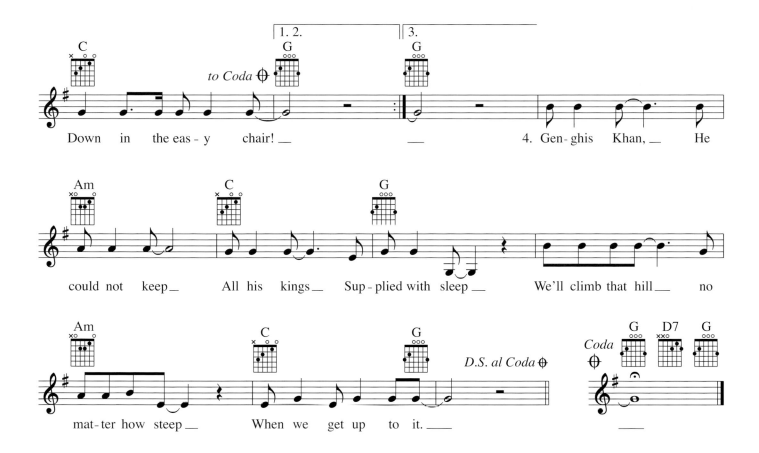

Down in the eas-y chair! __ __ 4. Gen-ghis Khan, __ He

could not keep__ All his kings__ Sup-plied with sleep __ We'll climb that hill__ no

mat-ter how steep__ When we get up to it. ___ ___

THIS WHEEL'S ON FIRE

The Basement Tapes, 1975

Written in collaboration with Rick Danko during the so-called 'basement tape' sessions of 1967, this song first reached the public via Julie Driscoll's hit cover version the following year. That was followed swiftly by Danko's own rendition with The Band on their debut LP, *Music From Big Pink*. Dylan's own interpretation was only released in 1975, and he didn't perform the song in concert until 1996. Driscoll and Ade Edmondson re-recorded a version of the song as the theme to the BBC sitcom *Absolutely Fabulous*, first aired in 1992.

"I was teaching myself to play piano. Some music I had written on the piano the day before just seemed to fit with Dylan's lyrics. Then Dylan and I wrote the chorus together."

Rick Danko

TEARS OF RAGE

The Basement Tapes, 1975

The second major composition co-written with a member of The Band during the 'basement tapes' era, 'Tears Of Rage' provided a memorable opening cut for their 1968 album, *Music From Big Pink*. Appropriately enough, Richard Manuel was the vocalist on that track, as he had written the melody for the song. Dylan's long awaited live premiere of the song finally occurred in 1989.

"Bob came down to the basement with a piece of type-written paper, and said, 'Have you got any music for this?'. I had a couple of musical movements that seemed to fit, so I just elaborated a little bit, because I wasn't sure what the lyrics meant. I couldn't run upstairs and say, 'What's this mean, Bob? "Now the heart is filled with gold as if it was a purse"?'"

Richard Manuel

TEARS OF RAGE

With Richard Manuel

Slowly

A   F♯m

We car-ried you   in our arms   On
point-ed out   the   way to go   And
all ver - y   pain - less   When you

D   Bm   G

In - de - pend - ence Day,   And now you'd throw us
scratched your name   in sand,   Though you just thought   it was
went out to   re - ceive   All that false   in -

D   A

all a - side   And put us on our way.   Oh
noth-ing more   Than a place for you to stand.   Now, I
struc - tion   Which we nev - er could be - lieve.   And

F♯m

what   dear daugh - ter   'neath the sun   Would
want you to know   that while we watched,   You dis -
now   the heart   is filled with gold   As

treat a fa - ther so,   To wait up - on ___ him
cov - er there was no one true.   Most ev - 'ry - bod - y
if it was ___ a purse.   But, oh, what kind ___ of

hand and foot ___   And al - ways tell him, "No?" ___
real - ly thought ___   It was a child-ish thing to do. ___
love is this ___   Which goes from bad to worse? ___

Tears of rage,   tears of grief, ___   Why must I al - ways
Tears of rage,   tears of grief, ___   Must I al - ways
Tears of rage,   tears of grief, ___   Must I al - ways

be the thief?   Come to me now, _ you know We're so a - lone
be the thief?   Come to me now, _ you know We're so ___ low
be the thief?   Come to me now, _ you know We're so ___ low

And life is brief.   We
And life is brief.   It was
And life is brief.

I DREAMED I SAW ST. AUGUSTINE

John Wesley Harding, 1967

With sparse accompaniment from bassist Charlie McCoy and drummer Kenny Buttrey, Dylan recorded this enigmatic song for the *John Wesley Harding* album in October 1967. He performed it with The Band at the 1969 Isle of Wight festival, shortly after his old friend Joan Baez included it on her album of Dylan covers, *Any Day Now*.

"*John Wesley Harding* was a fearful album – just dealing with fear, dealing with the devil in a fearful way, almost. All I wanted to do was to get the words right. It was courageous to do it."

Bob Dylan, 1978

I DREAMED I SAW ST. AUGUSTINE

Additional lyrics

2. "Arise, arise," he cried so loud
   In a voice without restraint
   "Come out, ye gifted kings and queens
   And hear my sad complaint
   No martyr is among ye now
   Whom you can call your own
   So go on your way accordingly
   But know you're not alone"

3. I dreamed I saw St. Augustine
   Alive with fiery breath
   And I dreamed I was amongst the ones
   That put him out to death
   Oh, I awoke in anger
   So alone and terrified
   I put my fingers against the glass
   And bowed my head and cried

ALL ALONG THE WATCHTOWER

John Wesley Harding, 1967

First issued on Dylan's *John Wesley Harding* album in December 1967, 'All Along The Watchtower' later became a rock anthem in the hands of Jimi Hendrix. Dylan's original recording was a gentler affair, cut in Nashville with a small band of the city's top sessionmen. He later reprised the song on his live albums *Before The Flood* and *Dylan & The Dead.*

"These songs on the *John Wesley Harding* album lack the traditional sense of time. 'All Along The Watchtower' opens up in a slightly different way, in a stranger way, because we have the cycle of events working in a rather reverse order."

Bob Dylan, 1968

DRIFTER'S ESCAPE

John Wesley Harding, 1967

Debuted in acoustic form on the *John Wesley Harding* album in 1967, 'Drifter's Escape' re-emerged in Dylan's live repertoire in the early 1990s as a muscular rock tune. Like 'All Along The Watchtower', it was a favourite of Jimi Hendrix, whose recording of the song was released soon after his death.

"A song has to be of a certain quality for me to sing and put on a record. One aspect it has to have is that it doesn't repeat itself."

Bob Dylan, 1968

DRIFTER'S ESCAPE

Moderately

"Oh,   help   me   in   my   weak -
judge,   he   cast   his   robe ___
stop   that   curs - ed   ju -

ness,"   I   heard   the   drift - er   say, ___
___ a - side, ___   A   tear   came   to   his   eye, ___
ry,"   Cried   the   at - tend - ant   and   the   nurse, ___

As   they   car - ried   him ___   from   the   court - room   And   were   tak -
"You   fail   to   un - der - stand," he said, ___ "Why   must ___
"The   trial   was   bad   e - nough,   But   this ___

ing   him   a - way. ___   "My   trip ___
___ you   e - ven   try?" ___   Out -
___ is   ten   times   worse." ___   Just   then ___

_____ has - n't been a pleas - ant one_ And my _____
side, the crowd was stir - ring, You could
_____ a bolt of light - ning_ Struck the

D **A**

_____ time it is - n't long, _____ And I _____
hear it from the door. _____ In - side, ___
court - house out of shape, ___ And while ev -

_3_

_____ still do not know_____ What it was ____ that I've done wrong."
_____ the judge was step - ping down, While the ju - ry cried for more. __
'ry - bod - y knelt to pray The drift - er did es - cape. __

D **A**

1.2. **3.**

_____ Well, the
_____ "Oh,
_____

I PITY THE POOR IMMIGRANT

John Wesley Harding, 1967

Dylan introduced this poignant tune as a tender acoustic ballad on 1967's *John Wesley Harding*. In 1976, he performed it in public for the first time in seven years with Joan Baez and the Rolling Thunder Revue, in a vibrant rock arrangement – a stunning demonstration of his unerring ability to recreate his own material in unexpected ways.

"Before I wrote *John Wesley Harding*, I discovered something about all those earlier songs I had written. I discovered that when I used words like 'he' and 'it' and 'they', I was really talking about nobody but me. I went into *John Wesley Harding* with that knowledge in my head."

Bob Dylan, 1970

I'LL BE YOUR BABY TONIGHT

John Wesley Harding, 1967

With Pete Drake's pedal steel adding an authentic Nashville flavour, 'I'll Be Your Baby Tonight' looked ahead to Dylan's country adventures to come when it was featured as the final track on 1967's *John Wesley Harding* album. He first performed it in concert at the Isle of Wight festival in August 1969.

"Maybe it was tongue-in-cheek, I don't know. It's just a simple song, a simple sentiment. I'd like to think it was written from a place where there is no struggle, but I'm probably wrong... sometimes you may be burning up inside but still do something that seems so cool and calm and collected."

Bob Dylan, 1985

DEAR LANDLORD

John Wesley Harding, 1967

'Dear Landlord' was the last song recorded for the *John Wesley Harding* album in November 1967. Charlie McCoy, Kenny Buttrey and Pete Drake provided the understated accompaniment. Joe Cocker transformed the song with an uptempo R&B arrangement for his 1969 cover version. Dylan finally debuted the song on stage during a concert in 1992.

"'Dear Landlord' was really just the first line. I woke up one morning with the words on my mind. Then I just figured, what else can I put to it?"

Bob Dylan, 1985

DEAR LANDLORD

Moderately slow

Dear land-lord, ___ Please don't ___ put a price on my

soul. My bur-den is heav-y, ___ My dreams are be-yond ___ con-

trol. ___ When that steam - boat whis - tle blows,

I'm gon - na give you all I got to give, ___ And I do hope you re -

ceive it well, ___ De-pend-in' on the way ___ you feel ___ that you

live. ___

2. Dear landlord
   Please heed these words that I speak
   I know you've suffered much
   But in this you are not so unique
   All of us, at times, we might work too hard
   To have it too fast and too much
   And anyone can fill his life up
   With things he can see but he just cannot touch

3. Dear landlord
   Please don't dismiss my case
   I'm not about to argue
   I'm not about to move to no other place
   Now, each of us has his own special gift
   And you know this was meant to be true
   And if you don't underestimate me
   I won't underestimate you

LAY, LADY, LAY

Nashville Skyline, 1969

Arguably the most popular song on Dylan's *Nashville Skyline* album, 'Lay Lady Lay' became a hit single in 1969, reaching the Top 10 in the UK and US. The familiar arrangement and lyrics were transformed by Dylan in 1976 for his performances with the Rolling Thunder Revue, as documented on the live album *Hard Rain*. Since then, the song has re-entered his live repertoire in more conventional form.

"*Nashville Skyline* is a very important album. He was getting away, getting back to his roots. His ballads are the finest things. What about 'Lay, Lady, Lay'? Could anyone else cover that?"

Eric Clapton

I THREW IT ALL AWAY

Nashville Skyline, 1969

Simple and deeply moving, 'I Threw It All Away' epitomised the easy grace of Dylan's 1969 venture into the heart of country music, *Nashville Skyline*. He performed the song that year on TV's *Johnny Cash Show*, and at the Isle of Wight festival. Seven years later, the song took on a much darker hue when it was included on the *Hard Rain* live album.

I THREW IT ALL AWAY

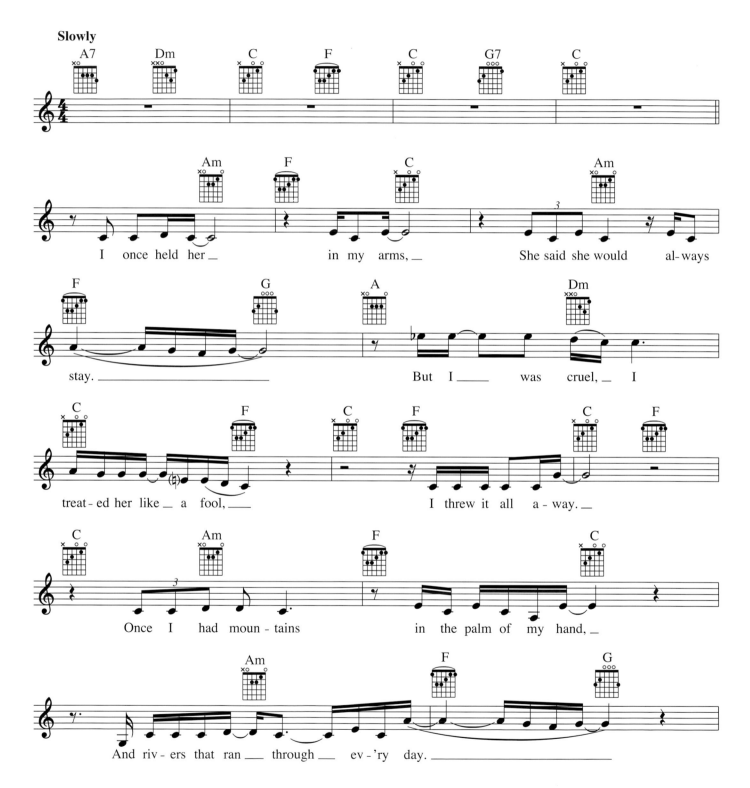

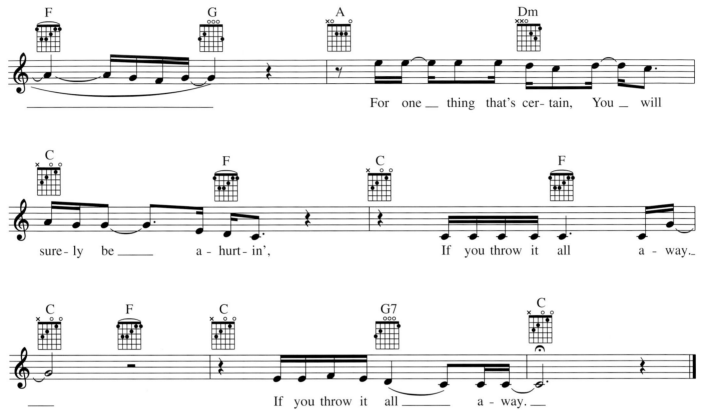

For one — thing that's cer- tain, You — will

sure- ly be _____ a - hurt- in', If you throw it all a - way.

_____ If you throw it all _____ a - way. __

"It's a song that we can all connect with. We all regret past relationships, which we've messed up. It's easy to sing that song."

Rob Snarski, The Blackeyed Susans

TONIGHT I'LL BE STAYING HERE WITH YOU

Nashville Skyline, 1969

'Tonight I'll Be Staying Here With You' was written at the Ramada Hotel in Nashville during the sessions for the *Nashville Skyline* album in February 1969. A minor hit single later that year, it entered the live arena (albeit in radically revised form) in 1975. Cher and Jeff Beck are among the other artists to have covered the song.

"That was a song which Bob wrote actually during the sessions, I seem to remember. One morning, he just came in with it, and we cut it right away. It was a beautiful song, very simple, but it cut right to the heart."

Charlie McCoy, bassist on Nashville Skyline

IF NOT FOR YOU

New Morning, 1970

This gentle country tune was recorded in the company of George Harrison during the 1970 sessions for the *New Morning* album. Harrison subsequently covered the song on *All Things Must Pass*, and his arrangement was utilised by Olivia Newton-John on her 1971 hit single. But it was only in 1992 that Dylan added the song to his own live repertoire.

be no-where at all,   Oh!___   What would I _____ do ____   If not ___ for you. _____

If   not   for   you, ____

Win - ter   would   have   no   spring, __   Could-n't hear the

rob - in   sing, __   I   just would-n't have a   clue, ___

An-y-way it would-n't ring   true, ___   If   not ___ for you. ___

repeat & fade

____   If   not   for ___ you. ___

282

"I wrote the song thinking about my wife. It seemed simple enough, sort of Tex-Mex. But I would never explore all the possibilities of instrumentation in the studio, add parts and so forth, or change the beat around, so it came off kind of folky."

Bob Dylan, 1985

NEW MORNING

New Morning, 1970

Recorded in June 1970, 'New Morning' became the title track of a
Bob Dylan album four months later. But the song had to wait more
than 20 years for a debut live performance. The original studio
take featured some of America's top session musicians, including
Al Kooper, Russ Kunkel, Charlie Daniels and Ron Cornelius.

This must be the day that   all   of   my __ dreams come   true __

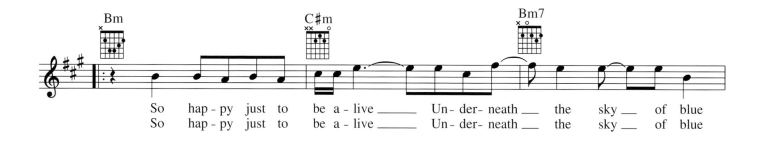

So   hap - py   just   to   be a - live _____ Un - der- neath __ the   sky __ of blue
So   hap - py   just   to   be a - live _____ Un - der- neath __ the   sky __ of blue

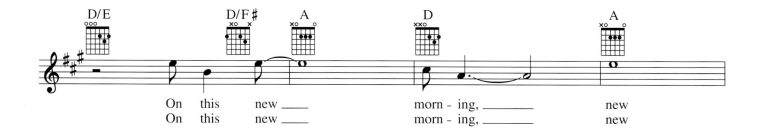

On   this   new _____   morn - ing, _____   new
On   this   new _____   morn - ing, _____   new

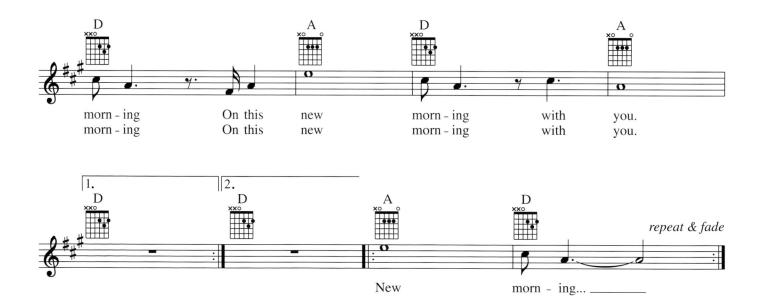

morn - ing   On this   new   morn - ing   with   you.
morn - ing   On this   new   morn - ing   with   you.

repeat & fade

New   morn - ing... _____

"A Broadway producer got hold of me. He wanted me to write the songs for an Archibald MacLeish play, called *The Devil and Daniel Webster*. Seemed like an interesting idea, so I recorded some stuff based on what he was doing, and I recorded 'New Morning'."

Bob Dylan, 1985

WATCHING THE RIVER FLOW

Bob Dylan's Greatest Hits, Vol. 2, 1971

One of two songs cut during some experimental 1971 sessions with Leon Russell and his band, 'Watching The River Flow' was issued as a single that summer, reaching the UK Top 30. It also appeared on the *More Greatest Hits* compilation at the end of that year. Dylan first performed the song in public in 1978, and it remains in his live repertoire to this day.

WATCHING THE RIVER FLOW

To sit down on _____ this bank of sand _____
But right now _____ I'll just sit here so con -

And watch the riv - er flow. _____
tent - ed - ly And watch the riv - er flow. _____

Peo - ple dis - a - gree - ing on all just a - bout ev - 'ry - thing, _____ yeah,
Peo - ple dis - a - gree - ing ev - ery - where you look, _____

Makes you stop and all _____ won - der why. _____ Why
Makes you wan - na stop _____ and read a book. Why

on - ly yes - ter - day I saw some-bod - y on the street _ Who just _____ could - n't help but
on - ly yes - ter - day I saw some-bod - y on the street _ That was _____

cry. Oh, _____ this ol' riv - er keeps on roll - in',
real - ly shook. _____ But this ol' riv - er keeps on roll - in',

though,   No mat -ter what gets in the way   and which way the
though,   No mat -ter what gets in the way   and which way the

wind does blow,   And as long _____ as it does   I'll   just
wind does blow,   And as long _____ as it does   I'll   just

sit here And watch _____ the riv - er flow. _
sit here And watch _____ the

riv - er flow. _   Watch the riv - er flow, _

Watch - in' the riv - er flow, _   Watch - in' the

riv - er flow, _   But I'll sit down on _____ this bank of ___

sand And watch the riv - er flow. _____

294

"We had this bet, that he could write a song right there and then. So I played him this track we had cut with my band, and then I watched him do it. He walked back and forth around the studio, and all these words started coming out."

Leon Russell

WHEN I PAINT MY MASTERPIECE

Bob Dylan's Greatest Hits, Vol. 2, 1971

Like 'Watching The River Flow', 'When I Paint My Masterpiece' was the product of a brief bout of recording with keyboardist/producer Leon Russell and his band. It was soon covered by The Band for their 1971 album *Cahoots*, and Dylan performed it with them at the end of that year. It later became his standard opening song during the 1975 Rolling Thunder Revue concerts.

"That was another song which he wrote with me there in the studio, watching him at work. That's where the chorus line came from – 'you'll be there with me when I paint my masterpiece'. And that was exactly where I was."

Leon Russell

KNOCKIN' ON HEAVEN'S DOOR

Pat Garrett and Billy the Kid, 1973

In November 1972, Bob Dylan travelled to Mexico to begin filming a role in Sam Peckinpah's movie, *Pat Garrett and Billy the Kid*. Contracted to provide the soundtrack music for the film, Dylan cut this heart-stoppingly poignant ballad in February 1973. It became a major hit single later that year, and has returned to the charts on several occasions since then, via covers by artists such as Eric Clapton and Guns 'N' Roses.

"It's such a great song, a very spiritual song."

Eric Clapton

KNOCKIN' ON HEAVEN'S DOOR

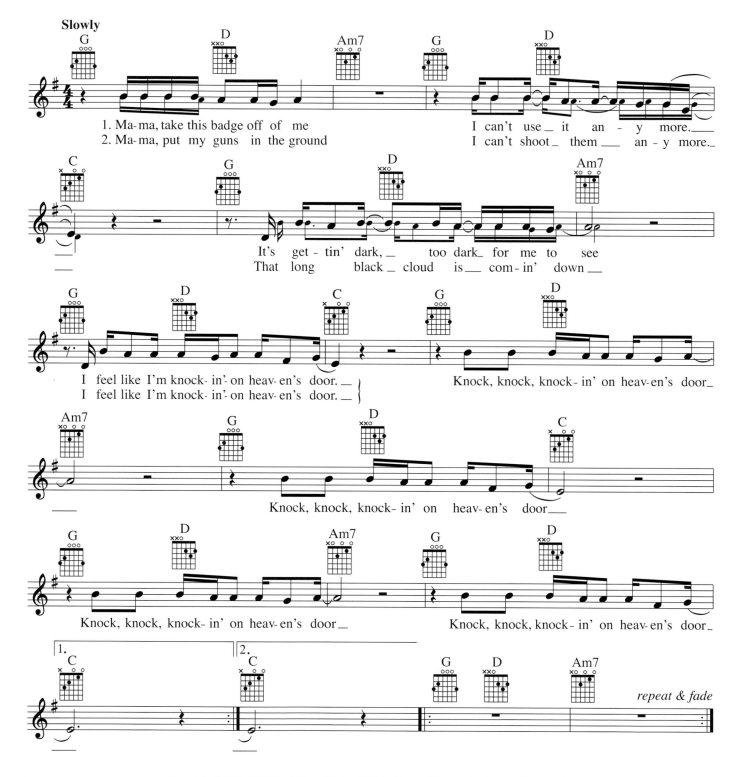

Slowly

1. Ma-ma, take this badge off of me   I can't use _ it an-y more.___
2. Ma-ma, put my guns in the ground   I can't shoot_ them ___ an-y more._

It's get-tin' dark, _ too dark_ for me to see
That long black_ cloud is_ com-in' down _

I feel like I'm knock-in'- on heav-en's door. _
I feel like I'm knock-in'- on heav-en's door. _

Knock, knock, knock-in' on heav-en's door_

Knock, knock, knock-in' on heav-en's door___

Knock, knock, knock-in' on heav-en's door_   Knock, knock, knock-in' on heav-en's door_

1.   2.

repeat & fade

"'Knockin' On Heaven's Door' is an extraordinary thing."

Allen Ginsberg

FOREVER YOUNG

Planet Waves, 1974

The anthemic 'Forever Young' was recorded in both acoustic and electric arrangements during the November 1973 sessions for the *Planet Waves* album. Unable to decide which version to include on the record, Dylan opted to use them both. An early demo recording of the song subsequently emerged on the *Biograph* compilation, while live performances can be found on *The Last Waltz* and *Bob Dylan At Budokan*.

have a strong _ foun - da - tion When the winds of chang - es shift. ____

May your heart al - ways be joy-ful, May your song al - ways be sung, May you

stay _____ for - ev - er young, _____ For - ev - er

young, _____ for - ev - er young, _____ May you

stay _____ for - ev - er young. _____

"'Forever Young' is a beautiful song. I've heard that sung round campfires, by people not recognizing it was Dylan, and when I told them, they'd say, 'Oh my God, that beautiful old favourite is Dylan?'."

Allen Ginsberg

TANGLED UP IN BLUE

Blood On The Tracks, 1975

Two starkly different readings of this remarkable song were taped for the *Blood On The Tracks* album. But Dylan still wasn't satisfied, rewriting the song for the stage and later announcing that it was the version captured on the 1984 album *Real Live* that represented the song's definitive incarnation. He has performed 'Tangled Up In Blue' at hundreds of concerts since then, often adjusting the lyrics along the way.

"That's one of the top ten songs of the 20th century."

Richard Thompson

4. She was workin' in a topless place
   And I stopped in for a beer
   I just kept lookin' at the side of her face
   In the spotlight so clear
   And later on as the crowd thinned out
   I's just about to do the same
   She was standing there in back of my chair
   Said to me, "Don't I know your name?"
   I muttered somethin' underneath my breath
   She studied the lines on my face
   I must admit I felt a little uneasy
   When she bent down to tie the laces of my shoe
   Tangled up in blue

5. She lit a burner on the stove and offered me a pipe
   "I thought you'd never say hello," she said
   "You look like the silent type"
   Then she opened up a book of poems
   And handed it to me
   Written by an Italian poet
   From the thirteenth century
   And every one of them words rang true
   And glowed like burnin' coal
   Pourin' off of every page
   Like it was written in my soul from me to you
   Tangled up in blue

6. I lived with them on Montague Street
   In a basement down the stairs
   There was music in the cafés at night
   And revolution in the air
   Then he started into dealing with slaves
   And something inside of him died
   She had to sell everything she owned
   And froze up inside
   And when finally the bottom fell out
   I became withdrawn
   The only thing I knew how to do
   Was to keep on keepin' on like a bird that flew
   Tangled up in blue

7. So now I'm goin' back again
   I got to get to her somehow
   All the people we used to know
   They're an illusion to me now
   Some are mathematicians
   Some are carpenter's wives
   Don't know how it all got started
   I don't know what they're doin' with their lives
   But me, I'm still on the road
   Headin' for another joint
   We always did feel the same
   We just saw it from a different point of view
   Tangled up in blue

"I was trying to do something that I didn't think had ever been done before – in terms of trying to tell a story and be a present character in it without it being some kind of fake, sappy, attempted tearjerker. I was trying to be somebody in the present time while conjuring up a lot of past images."

Bob Dylan, 1985

SIMPLE TWIST OF FATE

Blood On The Tracks, 1975

'Simple Twist Of Fate' was one of the ten superb songs that emerged from the 1974 recording sessions for the *Blood On The Tracks* album. Dylan subsequently rewrote many of the lyrics for a TV performance in honour of veteran producer John Hammond in September 1975. Joan Baez famously covered the song that year, devoting one verse to an impersonation of the song's composer.

2. A saxophone someplace far off played
   As she was walkin' by the arcade
   As the light bust through a beat-up shade where he was wakin' up
   She dropped a coin into the cup of a blind man at the gate
   And forgot about a simple twist of fate

   He woke up, the room was bare
   He didn't see her anywhere
   He told himself he didn't care, pushed the window open wide
   Felt an emptiness inside to which he just could not relate
   Brought on by a simple twist of fate

3. He hears the ticking of the clocks
   And walks along with a parrot that talks
   Hunts her down by the waterfront docks where the sailers all come in
   Maybe she'll pick him out again, how long must he wait
   Once more for a simple twist of fate

   People tell me it's a sin
   To know and feel too much within
   I still believe she was my twin, but I lost the ring
   She was born in spring, but I was born too late
   Blame it on a simple twist of fate

"If Dylan hadn't said some of the things he did, nobody else was going to say them. Can you imagine what a world it would be if we didn't have a Bob Dylan? It would be awful."

George Harrison

YOU'RE A BIG GIRL NOW

Blood On The Tracks, 1975

The tense emotional landscape of 'You're A Big Girl Now' was one of several songs intended for *Blood On The Tracks* that were re-recorded shortly before the album's January 1975 release date. An even more dramatic reading of the song surfaced a year later on the *Hard Rain* concert album.

"I read that this was supposed to be about my wife. I wish somebody would ask me first before they go ahead and print stuff like that. I mean, it couldn't be about anybody else but my wife, right? Stupid and misleading jerks."

Bob Dylan, 1985

YOU'RE A BIG GIRL NOW

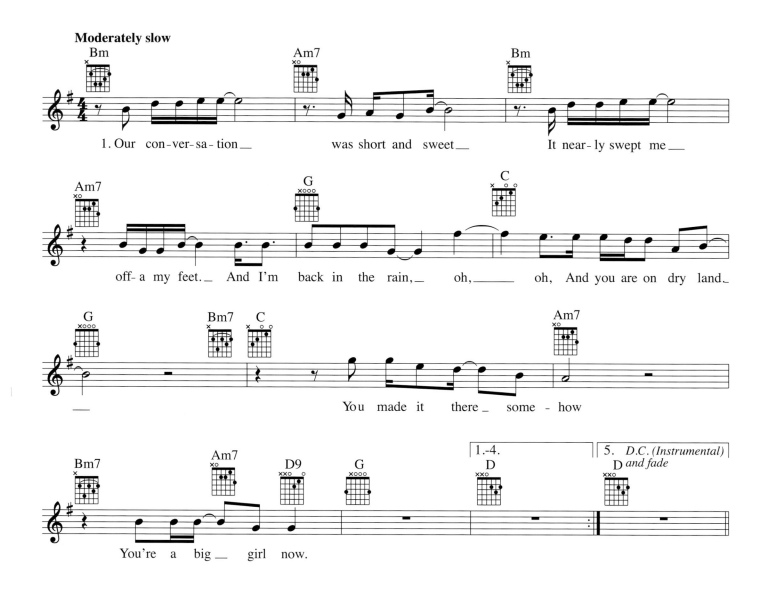

Moderately slow

1. Our con-ver-sa-tion _ was short and sweet _ It near-ly swept me _ off-a my feet. _ And I'm back in the rain, _ oh, _____ oh, And you are on dry land. _ _ You made it there _ some - how You're a big _ girl now.

1.-4.

5. *D.C. (Instrumental)* *and fade*

2. Bird on the horizon, sittin' on a fence
   He's singin' his song for me at his own expense
   And I'm just like that bird, oh, oh
   Singin' just for you
   I hope that you can hear
   Hear me singin' through these tears

3. Time is a jet plane, it moves too fast
   Oh, but what a shame if all we've shared can't last
   I can change, I swear, oh, oh
   See what you can do
   I can make it through
   You can make it too

4. Love is so simple, to quote a phrase
   You've known it all the time, I'm learnin' it these days
   Oh, I know where I can find you, oh, oh
   In somebody's room
   It's a price I have to pay
   You're a big girl all the way

5. A change in the weather is known to be extreme
   But what's the sense of changing horses in midstream?
   I'm going out of my mind, oh, oh
   With a pain that stops and starts
   Like a corkscrew to my heart
   Ever since we've been apart

IDIOT WIND

Blood On The Tracks, 1975

This tense, accusatory song was widely – but perhaps inaccurately – interpreted as being a raw slice of autobiography when it emerged on *Blood On The Tracks* in January 1975. The following year, a compelling live performance provided the highlight of the *Hard Rain* album. Dylan unexpectedly revived the tune during a run of concerts in 1992, but has not returned to it since then.

IDIOT WIND

Slowly, with a steady beat

1. Some-one's got it in ___ for me, they're plant-ing ___ sto - ries ___ in the ___ press

Who- ev - er it is ___ I wish they'd cut it out but when they will _____ I can on - ly

guess. ___ They say I shot a man ___ named Gray ___ and took his wife ___ to It - a - ly, _____

She in - her - it - ed a mil - lion bucks ___ and when she died ___ it came to me. ___ I can't

help it _____ if I'm luck- y. _____ Peo-ple see me all the time ___ and

they just can't re-mem - ber how to act _____ Their minds are filled with big ___ i - deas, _____

Additional lyrics

2. I ran into the fortune-teller, who said beware of lightning that might strike
   I haven't known peace and quiet for so long I can't remember what it's like
   There's a lone soldier on the cross, smoke pourin' out of a boxcar door
   You didn't know it, you didn't think it could be done, in the final end he won the wars
   After losin' every battle

   I woke up on the roadside, daydreamin' 'bout the way things sometimes are
   Visions of your chestnut mare shoot through my head and are makin' me see stars
   You hurt the ones that I love best and cover up the truth with lies
   One day you'll be in the ditch, flies buzzin' around your eyes
   Blood on your saddle

   Idiot wind, blowing through the flowers on your tomb
   Blowing through the curtains in your room
   Idiot wind, blowing every time you move your teeth
   You're an idiot, babe
   It's a wonder that you still know how to breathe

3. It was gravity which pulled us down and destiny which broke us apart
   You tamed the lion in my cage but it just wasn't enough to change my heart
   Now everything's a little upside down, as a matter of fact the wheels have stopped
   What's good is bad, what's bad is good, you'll find out when you reach the top
   You're on the bottom

   I noticed at the ceremony, your corrupt ways had finally made you blind
   I can't remember your face anymore, your mouth has changed, your eyes don't look into mine
   The priest wore black on the seventh day and sat stone-faced while the building burned
   I waited for you on the running boards, near the cypress trees, while the springtime turned
   Slowly into Autumn

   Idiot wind, blowing like a circle around my skull
   From the Grand Coulee Dam to the Capitol
   Idiot wind, blowing every time you move your teeth
   You're an idiot, babe
   It's a wonder that you still know how to breathe

4. I can't feel you anymore, I can't even touch the books you've read
   Every time I crawl past your door, I been wishin' I was somebody else instead
   Down the highway, down the tracks, down the road to ecstasy
   I followed you beneath the stars, hounded by your memory
   And all your ragin' glory

   I been double-crossed now for the very last time and now I'm finally free
   I kissed goodbye the howling beast on the borderline which separated you from me
   You'll never know the hurt I suffered nor the pain I rise above
   And I'll never know the same about you, your holiness or your kind of love
   And it makes me feel so sorry

   Idiot wind, blowing through the buttons of our coats
   Blowing through the letters that we wrote
   Idiot wind, blowing through the dust upon our shelves
   We're idiots, babe
   It's a wonder we can even feed ourselves

"That was a song I wanted to make as a painting. A lot of people thought that song, that album, *Blood On The Tracks*, pertained to me, because it seemed to at the time. It didn't pertain to me. It was just a concept of putting in images that defy time — yesterday, today and tomorrow. I wanted to make them all connect in some strange way."

Bob Dylan, 1985

IF YOU SEE HER, SAY HELLO

Blood On The Tracks, 1975

This intensely personal song was included on the remarkable song cycle that comprised the *Blood On The Tracks* album. A slightly earlier version was included on *The Bootleg Series Vols. 1-3* in 1991. Dylan has performed the song occasionally throughout his subsequent live career, often reworking the original lyrics.

"I love that — it's my favourite song."

Nick Cave

YOU'RE GONNA MAKE ME LONESOME WHEN YOU GO

Blood On The Tracks, 1975

This charmingly bittersweet portrayal of
romance was written in summer 1974 for
Dylan's epochal *Blood On The Tracks* album.
After featuring in the set-lists for his 1976 tour,
it has never been played in concert by Dylan
again. But the song deservedly reached a wider audience early
in the 21st century via Madeleine Peyroux's sensitive cover version.

"That's just a beautiful song. I always used to think – and this is a lesser
known part of his writing – that his romantic take on things always has
a very bittersweet quality. As far as I'm concerned, he writes the most
beautiful love songs, in a lot of ways, so that's why I was so excited
about recording that song."

Madeleine Peyroux

LILY, ROSEMARY AND THE JACK OF HEARTS

Blood On The Tracks, 1975

This lengthy narrative from the *Blood On The Tracks* album remains one of the most compelling items in Dylan's entire catalogue, its surreal storyline propelled by some immaculately tight musicianship. Sadly, the song never inspired the movie that its storyline demanded, and it only once surfaced in Dylan's concerts, in duet with Joan Baez during the second Rolling Thunder Revue tour.

11. The backstage manager was pacing all around by his chair
    "There's something funny going on," he said, "I can just feel it in the air"
    He went to get the hangin' judge, but the hangin' judge was drunk
    As the leading actor hurried by in the costume of a monk
    There was no actor anywhere better than the Jack of Hearts

12. Lily's arms were locked around the man that she dearly loved to touch
    She forgot all about the man she couldn't stand who hounded her so much
    "I've missed you so," she said to him, and he felt she was sincere
    But just beyond the door he felt jealousy and fear
    Just another night in the life of the Jack of Hearts

13. No one knew the circumstance but they say that it happened pretty quick
    The door to the dressing room burst open and a cold revolver clicked
    And Big Jim was standin' there, ya couldn't say surprised
    Rosemary right beside him, steady in her eyes
    She was with Big Jim but she was leanin' to the Jack of Hearts

14. Two doors down the boys finally made it through the wall
    And cleaned out the bank safe, it's said that they got off with quite a haul
    In the darkness by the riverbed they waited on the ground
    For one more member who had business back in town
    But they couldn't go no further without the Jack of Hearts

15. The next day was hangin' day, the sky was overcast and black
    Big Jim lay covered up, killed by a penknife in the back
    And Rosemary on the gallows, she didn't even blink
    The hangin' judge was sober, he hadn't had a drink
    The only person on the scene missin' was the Jack of Hearts

16. The cabaret was empty now, a sign said, "Closed for repair"
    Lily had already taken all of the dye out of her hair
    She was thinkin' 'bout her father, who she very rarely saw
    Thinkin' 'bout Rosemary and thinkin' about the law
    But, most of all she was thinkin' 'bout the Jack of Hearts

"He understood folk music's capacity and its storytelling power. It wasn't formulaic. He saw how folk was able to inform timeless messages. His talent was so palpable, you could feel it."

Paul Stookey, one-third of folk trio Peter, Paul & Mary

SHELTER FROM THE STORM

Blood On The Tracks, 1975

'Shelter From The Storm' was recorded during the initial batch of sessions for the *Blood On The Tracks* album in September 1974. In 1976, it featured regularly during the second Rolling Thunder Revue tour, and an electrifying rendition (with Dylan playing slide guitar) was included in the *Hard Rain* TV special and live album. The song subsequently appeared on the *Bob Dylan At Budokan* set in 1978, and has been performed countless times since then.

al - ways do my best ____ for her, on that I give ____ my word ____
Poi - soned in the bush - es an' blown out on ____ the trail, ____
took too much for grant - ed, got my sig - nals crossed. ____
old men with bro - ken teeth strand - ed with - out love. ____
Beau - ty walks a ra - zor's edge, some - day I'll make it mine. ____

____
____ In a world of steel - eyed death, and men ____ who are
____ Hunt - ed like a croc - o - dile, ____
____ Do I Just to think that it all be - gan ____ on a
____ Do I un - der - stand your ques - tion, man, ____ is it
____ If I could on - ly turn back the clock ____ to when

fight - ing to be warm. ____
rav - aged in the corn. ____
long - for - got - ten morn. ____   "Come in," she said, "I'll give ____
hope - less and for - lorn? ____
God and her were born. ____

____ you shel - ter from ____ the storm."

1.-4.   5.

2. Not a
3. Sud - den -
4. Well, the
5. In a

"I love the beautiful complexity of his images. He uses very specific images and melds them into his melody so that it all sounds like first inspiration. The greatest artists do that. The song feels like they reflect your own life back to you."

Rosanne Cash

HURRICANE

Desire, 1976

After visiting imprisoned boxer Rubin 'Hurricane' Carter in jail during the summer of 1975, Dylan and his co-writer Jacques Levy penned this cinematic account of the circumstances which had led to his arrest – unjustly, or so Carter claimed. The song kicked-off Dylan's Desire album, and was performed with the Rolling Thunder Revue during their late 1975 tour.

6. Four months later, the ghettos are in flame
   Rubin's in South America, fightin' for his name
   While Arthur Dexter Bradley's still in the robbery game
   And the cops are puttin' the screws to him, lookin' for somebody to blame
   "Remember that murder that happened in a bar?"
   "Remember you said you saw the getaway car?"
   "You think you'd like to play ball with the law?"
   "Think it might-a been that fighter that you saw runnin' that night?"
   "Don't forget that you are white"

7. Arthur Dexter Bradley said, "I'm really not sure"
   Cops said, "A poor boy like you could use a break
   We got you for the motel job and we're talkin' to your friend Bello
   Now you don't wanta have to go back to jail, be a nice fellow
   You'll be doin' society a favor
   That sonofabitch is brave and gettin' braver
   We want to put his ass in stir
   We want to pin this triple murder on him
   He ain't no Gentleman Jim"

8. Rubin could take a man out with just one punch
   But he never did like to talk about it all that much
   It's my work, he'd say, and I do it for pay
   And when it's over I'd just as soon go on my way
   Up to some paradise
   Where the trout streams flow and the air is nice
   And ride a horse along a trail
   But then they took him to the jailhouse
   Where they try to turn a man into a mouse

9. All of Rubin's cards were marked in advance
   The trial was a pig-circus, he never had a chance
   The judge made Rubin's witnesses drunkards from the slums
   To the white folks who watched he was a revolutionary bum
   And to the black folks he was just a crazy nigger
   No one doubted that he pulled the trigger
   And though they could not produce the gun
   The D.A. said he was the one who did the deed
   And the all-white jury agreed

10. Rubin Carter was falsely tried
    The crime was murder "one," guess who testified?
    Bello and Bradley and they both baldly lied
    And the newspapers, they all went along for the ride
    How can the life of such a man
    Be in the palm of some fool's hand?
    To see him obviously framed
    Couldn't help but make me feel ashamed to live in a land
    Where justice is a game

11. Now all the criminals in their coats and their ties
    Are free to drink martinis and watch the sun rise
    While Rubin sits like Buddha in a ten-foot cell
    An innocent man in a living hell
    That's the story of the Hurricane
    But it won't be over till they clear his name
    And give him back the time he's done
    Put in a prison cell, but one time he could-a been
    The champion of the world

"Hurricane sent me his book, which I read and which really touched me. I felt that the man was just innocent, from his writings and knowing that part of the country. So I went to visit him and was really behind him, trying to get a new trial."

Bob Dylan, 1985

ISIS

Desire, 1976

The focus of an extraordinary concert sequence in Dylan's movie *Renaldo & Clara*, 'Isis' was written with Jacques Levy during the summer 1975 sessions for the *Desire* album. The song featured prominently throughout the two Rolling Thunder Revue tours, but Dylan has not performed it in concert since 1976.

"It was just extraordinary, the two of us started to get hot together. We began to work on this thing and we just kept going with it, and we'd stop, and we didn't know where the story was going to go next. We were just having a great time laughing and coming up with one verse after another, and we kept on going until five in the morning, and we finished the song. And both of us thought it was great."

Jacques Levy

ONE MORE CUP OF COFFEE

Desire, 1976

Co-written with Jacques Levy, 'One More Cup Of Coffee' featured on the Desire album, the Rolling Thunder tour, and the Renaldo & Clara movie. Dylan continued to perform the song occasionally until the early 1990s.

"It's a gypsy song. That song was written during a gypsy festival in the south of France one summer. Somebody took me to a birthday party there once, and hanging out there for a week probably influenced the writing of that song. But the 'valley below' probably came from some place else."

Bob Dylan, 1991

OH, SISTER

Desire, 1976

One of the most poignant songs in Dylan's catalogue, 'Oh Sister'
was cut during the remarkable spontaneous sessions for the *Desire*
album in July 1975. Emmylou Harris was the vocalist presented
with the challenge of harmonising with Dylan's lead, with the barest
minimum of rehearsals. For the next three years, Dylan performed
'Oh Sister' regularly in concert, but it vanished from his set-lists in
July 1978.

"I would have been very intimidated, except that we just got right
down to work, and the work was reading the lyrics off the page.
We were cutting the song, watching him and trying to phrase with
him while not really knowing the song. It was all live. It was like a
painter that works by just throwing paint up on the canvas and yet
there's this real method to his madness. He knew what he was doing.
It was an extraordinary experience."

Emmylou Harris

ROMANCE IN DURANGO

Desire, 1976

This cowboy-movie drama, co-written with playwright Jacques Levy
for the *Desire* album, was perhaps partly inspired by Dylan's
experiences in Mexico on the set of *Pat Garrett and Billy The Kid.*
The song fully came into its own on the first Rolling Thunder
Revue tour in 1975, as documented in another movie, the
Dylan-directed *Renaldo & Clara.* It reappeared unexpectedly in
his live repertoire for a triumphant London performance in 2003.

2. Past the Aztec ruins and the ghosts of our people
   Hoofbeats like castanets on stone
   At night I dream of bells in the village steeple
   Then I see the bloody face of Ramon

   Was it me that shot him down in the cantina
   Was it my hand that held the gun?
   Come, let us fly, my Magdalena
   The dogs are barking and what's done is done

   Refrain

3. At the corrida we'll sit in the shade
   And watch the young torero stand alone
   We'll drink tequila where our grandfathers stayed
   When they rode with Villa into Torreón

   Then the padre will recite the prayers of old
   In the little church this side of town
   I will wear new boots and an earring of gold
   You'll shine with diamonds in your wedding gown

   The way is long but the end is near
   Already the fiesta has begun
   The face of God will appear
   With His serpent eyes of obsidian

   Refrain

4. Was that the thunder that I heard?
   My head is vibrating, I feel a sharp pain
   Come sit by me, don't say a word
   Oh, can it be that I am slain?

   Quick, Magdalena, take my gun
   Look up in the hills, that flash of light
   Aim well my little one
   We may not make it through the night

   Refrain

"The first thing that came was an image I had from a postcard that was once sent to me… with a picture of a Mexican hacienda, or something – some Mexican shack – a shack with a bunch of chilli peppers on the roof in the sun. So the first line was 'Hot chilli peppers in the sun', and I remember saying, 'No, blistering sun', so we had the first line."

Jacques Levy

SEÑOR (TALES OF YANKEE POWER)

Street Legal, 1978

The *Street Legal* album was recorded in spring 1978, during a brief pause in the most extensive world tour of Dylan's entire career. 'Señor' was debuted two weeks before the album reached the shops, in a concert at the Universal Amphitheatre in Hollywood on 1 June 1978. It remained in his set as he reached Europe for his first tour of the continent in 12 years, and he has continued to perform the song ever since.

"'Señor' was one of them border type things… sort of lost Yankee on gloomy Sunday, carnival type of thing… I see this as the aftermath of when two people who were leaning on each other because neither one of them had the guts to stand up alone, all of a sudden they break apart."

Bob Dylan, 1985

GOTTA SERVE SOMEBODY

Slow Train Coming, 1979

The release of the *Slow Train Coming* album marked a radical new direction in Bob Dylan's work. 'Gotta Serve Somebody' was the opening track, cut at the legendary Muscle Shoals Sound Studio in Alabama in May 1979. The song won him a Grammy Award for the first time, for the Best Male Rock Vocal Performance of 1979.

"Me like his song 'Serve Somebody' quite a bit. I glad he do it, too, y'know, because there comes a time when an artist just cannot follow the crowd. If you are an artist like Bob Dylan, you got to make the crowd follow you."

Bob Marley

GOTTA SERVE SOMEBODY

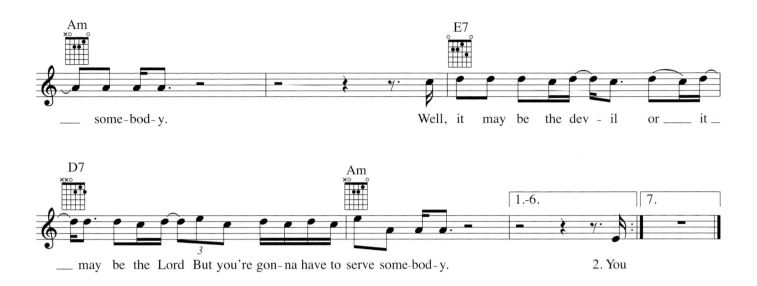

some-bod-y. Well, it may be the dev-il or __ it __ may be the Lord But you're gon-na have to serve some-bod-y. 2. You

Additional lyrics

2. You might be a rock 'n' roll addict prancing on the stage
   You might have drugs at your command, women in a cage
   You may be a business man or some high-degree thief
   They may call you Doctor or they may call you Chief

   But you're gonna have to serve somebody, yes indeed
   You're gonna have to serve somebody
   Well, it may be the devil or it may be the Lord
   But you're gonna have to serve somebody

3. You may be a state trooper, you might be a young Turk
   You may be the head of some big TV network
   You may be rich or poor, you may be blind or lame
   You may be living in another country under another name

   But you're gonna have to serve somebody, yes indeed
   You're gonna have to serve somebody
   Well, it may be the devil or it may be the Lord
   But you're gonna have to serve somebody

4. You may be a construction worker working on a home
   You may be living in a mansion or you might live in a dome
   You might own guns and you might even own tanks
   You might be somebody's landlord, you might even own
      banks

   But you're gonna have to serve somebody, yes indeed
   You're gonna have to serve somebody
   Well, it may be the devil or it may be the Lord
   But you're gonna have to serve somebody

5. You may be a preacher with your spiritual pride
   You may be a city councilman taking bribes on the side
   You may be workin' in a barbershop, you may know how to
      cut hair
   You may be somebody's mistress, may be somebody's heir

   But you're gonna have to serve somebody, yes indeed
   You're gonna have to serve somebody
   Well, it may be the devil or it may be the Lord
   But you're gonna have to serve somebody

6. Might like to wear cotton, might like to wear silk
   Might like to drink whiskey, might like to drink milk
   You might like to eat caviar, you might like to eat bread
   You may be sleeping on the floor, sleeping in a king-sized bed

   But you're gonna have to serve somebody, yes indeed
   You're gonna have to serve somebody
   Well, it may be the devil or it may be the Lord
   But you're gonna have to serve somebody

7. You may call me Terry, you may call me Timmy
   You may call me Bobby, you may call me Zimmy
   You may call me R.J., you may call me Ray
   You may call me anything but no matter what you say

   You're gonna have to serve somebody, yes indeed
   You're gonna have to serve somebody
   Well, it may be the devil or it may be the Lord
   But you're gonna have to serve somebody

I BELIEVE IN YOU

Slow Train Coming, 1979

One of Dylan's most comprehensive expressions of his religious faith, 'I Believe In You' appeared on the 1979 album *Slow Train Coming.* He regularly returned to the song in concert in the late 1980s and early 1990s, and again in the 21st century.

SAVING GRACE

🎵 *Saved*, 1980

Dylan's ability to confound his critics and his public was perfectly illustrated by the furore that surrounded his *Slow Train Coming* and *Saved* albums. The controversy masked the power of some of his finest material, not least this superb gospel ballad from 1980's *Saved*, which was enriched by some of Dylan's most emotional harmonica playing.

4. Well, the devil's shining light, it can be most blinding
   But to search for love, that ain't no more than vanity
   As I look around this world all that I'm finding
   Is the saving grace that's over me

5. The wicked know no peace and you just can't fake it
   There's only one road and it leads to Calvary
   It gets discouraging at times, but I know I'll make it
   By the saving grace that's over me

"People came to me when he put out his Christian records and said, 'This guy's finished – he can't speak to us anymore'. I thought those were some of the most beautiful gospel songs that have ever entered the whole landscape of gospel music."

Leonard Cohen

EVERY GRAIN OF SAND

Shot Of Love, 1981

One of Dylan's most lyrical ballads, 'Every Grain Of Sand' was recorded in May 1981 for his *Shot Of Love* album. A demo performance taped eight months earlier was released on the 1991 retrospective collection, *The Bootleg Series Volumes 1–3*.

"That's a good poem set to music. It's a beautiful melody, too, isn't it?"

Bob Dylan, 1991

EVERY GRAIN OF SAND

Moderately slow, in 2

1. In the
time of my con - fes - sion, in the hour of my deep - est need __
flow - ers of in - dul - gence and the weeds of yes - ter - year, __

__ When the pool of tears be - neath my feet flood ev - ery new - born __
__ Like crim - 'nals they have choked the breath of con - science and good __

seed. There's a dy - in' voice with - in me reach - ing out some -
cheer. The __ sun - beat down up - on the steps of time to light the

where, Toil - ing in the dan - ger and in the mor - als __ of __ de -
way To ease the pain of i - dle - ness and the mem - o - ry __ of __ de -

spair.   Don't have   the   in - cli - na - tion   to look   back   on an - y mis -
cay.   I   gaze   in - to   the   door-way   of temp - ta - tion's an - gry __

take,   Like   Cain,   I   now   be - hold   this chain of   e - vents   that   I ____ must
flame   And   ev - ery   time   I   pass   that   way   I   al - ways hear __ my

break.   In   the   fu - ry ____ of   the   mo - ment   I   can   see   the   Mas - ter's
name.   Then   on - ward __ in   my   jour-ney   I   come   to   un - der -

hand   In   ev - ery   leaf   that   trem - bles,   in   ev - ery   grain __ of
stand   That   ev - ery   hair   is   num - bered   like   ev - ery   grain __ of

1.   **2.**

sand.   2. Oh, the   sand.   3. I   have

gone   from rags   to   rich - es   in   the   sor - row   of   the   night   In   the

"'Every Grain Of Sand' was an excellent song, a very painless song to write. It took like 12 seconds – or that's how it felt."

Bob Dylan, 1992

JOKERMAN

Infidels, 1983

Arguably the brightest gem from the Mark Knopfler-produced *Infidels* album, 'Jokerman' went through a series of revisions in the early 1980s to emerge as the opening track – and the subject of one of Dylan's earliest promotional videos. It was the first song performed on his 1984 tour, and regularly opened his shows in 1994 as well.

2. So swiftly the sun sets in the sky
   You rise up and say goodbye to no one
   Fools rush in where angels fear to tread
   Both of their futures, so full of dread, you don't show one
   Shedding off one more layer of skin
   Keeping one step ahead of the persecutor within

   Refrain

3. You're a man of the mountains, you can walk on the clouds
   Manipulator of crowds, you're a dream twister
   You're going to Sodom and Gomorrah
   But what do you care? Ain't nobody there would want to marry your sister
   Friend to the martyr, a friend to the woman of shame
   You look into the fiery furnace, see the rich man without any name

   Refrain

4. Well, the Book of Leviticus and Deuteronomy
   The law of the jungle and the sea are your only teachers
   In the smoke of the twilight on a milk-white steed
   Michelangelo indeed could've carved out your features
   Resting in the fields, far from the turbulent space
   Half asleep near the stars with a small dog licking your face

   Refrain

5. Well, the rifleman's stalking the sick and the lame
   Preacherman seeks the same, who'll get there first is uncertain
   Nightsticks and water cannons, tear gas, padlocks
   Molotov cocktails and rocks behind every curtain
   False-hearted judges dying in the webs that they spin
   Only a matter of time 'til night comes steppin' in

   Refrain

6. It's a shadowy world, skies are slippery gray
   A woman just gave birth to a prince today and dressed him in scarlet
   He'll put the priest in his pocket, put the blade to the heat
   Take the motherless children off the street
   And place them at the feet of a harlot
   Oh, Jokerman, you know what he wants
   Oh, Jokerman, you don't show any response

   Refrain

"'Jokerman' came to me in the [Caribbean] islands. It's very mystical. The shapes there, and shadows, seem to be so ancient."

Bob Dylan, 1984

BLIND WILLIE MCTELL

Infidels, 1983

Inspired by the blues standard 'St. James Infirmary', Dylan composed this song during the 1983 sessions for his *Infidels* album. He experimented with two different arrangements before deciding to omit it from the finished record. But 'Blind Willie McTell' did finally see the light of day on the retrospective box set, *The Bootleg Series Volumes 1–3*, in 1991.

I'm gaz-ing out__ the win - dow_____ Of the St. James Hot-el,_____

And I know no one__ can sing the blues_____ Like Blind Wil - lie____ Mc - Tell.____

Instrumental

rit.

2. Well, I heard that hoot owl singing
   As they were taking down the tents
   The stars above the barren trees
   Was his only audience
   Them charcoal gypsy maidens
   Can strut their feathers well
   But nobody can sing the blues
   Like Blind Willie McTell

4. There's a woman by the river
   With some fine young handsome man
   He's dressed up like a squire
   Bootlegged whiskey in his hand
   There's a chain gang on the highway
   I can hear them rebels yell
   And I know no one can sing the blues
   Like Blind Willie McTell

"I started playing it live because I heard The Band doing it. Most likely it was a demo, probably showing the musicians how it should go. It was never developed fully, I never got around to completing it. There wouldn't have been any other reason for leaving it off the record."

Bob Dylan, 2006

BROWNSVILLE GIRL

Knocked Out Loaded, 1986

The product of a one-off songwriting collaboration with playwright Sam Shepard, the epic 'Brownsville Girl' began life under the guise of 'New Danville Girl' during the 1985 sessions for Dylan's *Empire Burlesque*. After lyrical revisions, it emerged a year later on the *Knocked Out Loaded* album.

7. Well, we crossed the panhandle and then we headed towards Amarillo
We pulled up where Henry Porter used to live. He owned a wreckin' lot outside of town about a mile
Ruby was in the backyard hanging clothes, she had her red hair tied back
She saw us come rolling up in a trail of dust
She said, "Henry ain't here but you can come on in, he'll be back in a little while"

8. Then she told us how times were tough and about how she was thinkin' of bummin' a ride back to from where she started
But ya know, she changed the subject every time money came up
She said, "Welcome to the land of the living dead." You could tell she was so broken hearted
She said, "Even the swap meets around here are getting pretty corrupt"

9. "How far are y'all going?" Ruby asked us with a sigh
"We're going all the way 'til the wheels fall off and burn
'Til the sun peels the paint and the seat covers fade and the water moccasin dies"
Ruby just smiled and said, "Ah, you know some babies never learn"

10. Something about that movie though, well I just can't get it out of my head
But I can't remember why I was in it or what part I was supposed to play
All I remember about it was Gregory Peck and the way people moved
And a lot of them seemed to be lookin' my way

Refrain

11. Well, they were looking for somebody with a pompadour
I was crossin' the street when shots rang out
I didn't know whether to duck or to run, so I ran
"We got him cornered in the churchyard," I heard somebody shout

12. Well, you saw my picture in the *Corpus Christi Tribune*. Underneath it, it said, "A man with no alibi"
You went out on a limb to testify for me, you said I was with you
Then when I saw you break down in front of the judge and cry real tears
It was the best acting I saw anybody do

13. Now I've always been the kind of person that doesn't like to trespass but sometimes you just find yourself over the line
Oh if there's an original thought out there, I could use it right now
You know, I feel pretty good, but that ain't sayin' much. I could feel a whole lot better
If you were just here by my side to show me how

14. Well, I'm standin' in line in the rain to see a movie starring Gregory Peck
Yeah, but you know it's not the one that I had in mind
He's got a new one out now, I don't even know what it's about
But I'll see him in anything so I'll stand in line

Refrain

15. You know, it's funny how things never turn out the way you had 'em planned
The only thing we knew for sure about Henry Porter is that his name wasn't Henry Porter
And you know there was somethin' about you baby that I liked that was always too good for this world
Just like you always said there was somethin' about me you liked that I left behind in the French Quarter

16. Strange how people who suffer together have stronger connections than people who are most content
I don't have any regrets, they can talk about me plenty when I'm gone
You always said people don't do what they believe in, they just do what's most convenient, then they repent
And I always said, "Hang on to me, baby, and let's hope that the roof stays on"

17. There was a movie I seen one time, I think I sat through it twice
I don't remember who I was or where I was bound
All I remember about it was it starred Gregory Peck, he wore a gun and he was shot in the back
Seems like a long time ago, long before the stars were torn down

Refrain

"It has to do with a guy standing on line and waiting to see an old Gregory Peck movie that he can't quite remember – only pieces of it – and this whole memory thing happens, unfolding before his very eyes. He starts speaking internally to a woman, reliving the whole journey they'd gone on. We spent two days writing the lyrics."

Sam Shepard

RING THEM BELLS

💿 *Oh Mercy*, 1989

After its initial appearance on *Oh Mercy* in 1989, 'Ring Them Bells' emerged as one of Dylan's most effective vehicles in concert – and rarely performed better than at the globally-televised Great Music Experience festival from Japan in 1994. Joan Baez also utilized the song as the title track of a 1990s album.

"It's mysterious and dark… Some of the songs on this record are the best songs I've heard in a while. And his voice sounds very sensuous. He's such a fine lyricist and craftsman with words. He's staggering, the concentration that he has for lyrics."

Daniel Lanois, producer of *Oh Mercy*

MOST OF THE TIME

Oh Mercy, 1989

This emotionally compelling song was one of the highlights of 1989's *Oh Mercy* album. Dylan subsequently recorded a second version for a promotional video, and performed the song sporadically in concert over the next three years.

"I think he's amazingly sensitive to all kinds of outside experience, the same as any artist who is really good at something. His songs take us to another level. He is absolutely a poet. He made songwriting into an art form, and made it worthy of committing your soul to."

Kris Kristofferson

MAN IN THE LONG BLACK COAT

🎵 *Oh Mercy, 1989*

This faintly chilling portrait was recorded in spring 1989 for the *Oh Mercy* album, produced by Daniel Lanois in New Orleans. He added the song to his stage repertoire that October, and it remains one of his most effective concert showcases.

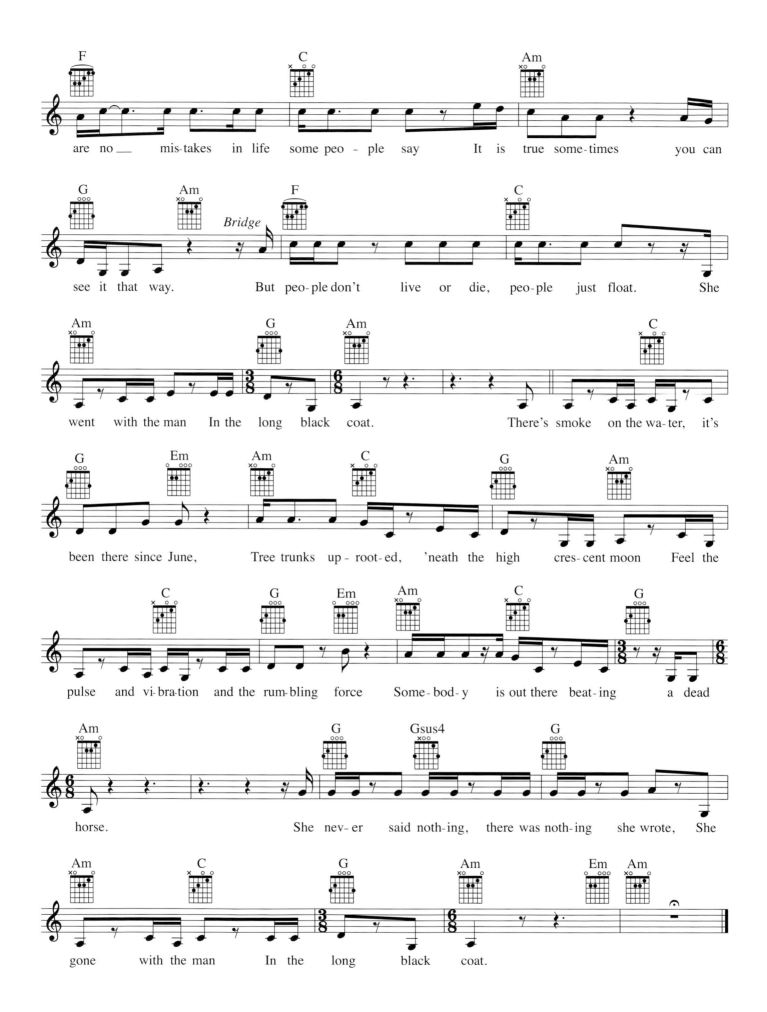

are no — mis-takes in life some peo - ple say It is true some-times you can

see it that way. But peo-ple don't live or die, peo-ple just float. She

went with the man In the long black coat. There's smoke on the wa-ter, it's

been there since June, Tree trunks up - root-ed, 'neath the high cres-cent moon Feel the

pulse and vi-bra-tion and the rum-bling force Some-bod-y is out there beat-ing a dead

horse. She nev-er said noth-ing, there was noth-ing she wrote, She

gone with the man In the long black coat.

"It's one of my favourites.
It paints a picture of small town
Americana, a dance hall on the
outskirts of town, and how a
strange individual comes in, and
'Not a word of goodbye, not
even a note, she's gone with the
man in the long black coat'."

Daniel Lanois

DIGNITY

Bob Dylan's Greatest Hits, Vol. 3, 1994

Although it was originally earmarked for the 1989 album *Oh Mercy*, 'Dignity' remained in the vaults until 1994, when it was overdubbed and remixed for the compilation album *Bob Dylan's Greatest Hits Vol. 3*. It subsequently became a highlight of his MTV Unplugged concert, and this performance reached the UK Top 40 singles chart in 1995.

2. Blind man breakin' out of a trance
   Puts both his hands in the pockets of chance
   Hopin' to find one circumstance
   Of dignity

   I went to the wedding of Mary Lou
   She said "I don't want nobody see me talkin' to you"
   Said she could get killed if she told me what she knew
   About dignity

   I went down where the vultures feed
   I would've gone deeper, but there wasn't any need
   Heard the tongues of angels and the tongues of men
   Wasn't any difference to me

   Chilly wind sharp as a razor blade
   House on fire, debts unpaid
   Gonna stand at the window, gonna ask the maid
   Have you seen dignity?

3. Drinkin' man listens to the voice he hears
   In a crowded room full of covered up mirrors
   Lookin' into the lost forgotten years
   For dignity

   Met Prince Phillip at the home of the blues
   Said he'd give me information if his name wasn't used
   He wanted money up front, said he was abused
   By dignity

   Footprints runnin' cross the silver sand
   Steps goin' down into tattoo land
   I met the sons of darkness and the sons of light
   In the bordertowns of despair

   Got no place to fade, got no coat
   I'm on the rollin' river in a jerkin' boat
   Tryin' to read a note somebody wrote
   About dignity

4. Sick man lookin' for the doctor's cure
   Lookin' at his hands for the lines that were
   And into every masterpiece of literature
   For dignity

   Englishman stranded in the blackheart wind
   Combin' his hair back, his future looks thin
   Bites the bullet and he looks within
   For dignity

   Someone showed me a picture and I just laughed
   Dignity never been photographed
   I went into the red, went into the black
   Into the valley of dry bone dreams

   So many roads, so much at stake
   So many dead ends, I'm at the edge of the lake
   Sometimes I wonder what it's gonna take
   To find dignity

"People can learn everything
about me through my songs,
if they know where to look."

Bob Dylan, 1990

SERIES OF DREAMS

The Bootleg Series Volumes 1–3, 1991

The release of *The Bootleg Series Vols. 1–3* confirmed what Dylan fans had long suspected, that the man had amassed a remarkable catalogue of unreleased material. Foremost amongst the unheard songs was this exhibition of sustained lyrical genius, considered for the *Oh Mercy* album but omitted from the final running order.

"'Series Of Dreams' was a fantastic turbulent track that I felt should have been on the record [*Oh Mercy*]. But Dylan had the final word."

Daniel Lanois, producer of *Oh Mercy*

SERIES OF DREAMS

With a moving beat

1. I was
2. *See ad-*

think-ing __ of a se-ries of __ dreams Where
ditional lyrics

noth-ing comes up to the top Eve-ry-thing

stays down where it's wound-ed And comes

to a per-ma-nent stop Was-n't think-ing

of an-y-thing spe-cif-ic Like in a dream, when

some-one wakes up and screams   Noth-ing   too ver-y sci-en-

tif - ic   Just think-ing   of a se-ries of ___

1. C   Csus4   C   Csus4   **2.** C   Am

dreams   dreams   Dreams where

F   C   Csus4   C   Am

the um-brel-la is fold-ed   In - to

F   C   Am

the path you are hurled   And the cards are

F   C

no good that you're hold-ing   Un - less they're

G   C   G

from an-oth-er world   3. In one,   num-bers were

LOVE SICK

🎵 *Time Out Of Mind*, 1997

This brooding essay on romantic disillusion provided a suitably atmospheric opening to the long-awaited 1997 album, *Time Out Of Mind*, Dylan's first album of new original material in seven years. He debuted the song in concert the night before the album was released, and performed it at the Grammy Awards ceremony the following year.

Additional lyrics

3. I see, I see lovers in the meadow
   I see, I see silhouettes in the window
   I watch them 'til they're gone and they leave me hanging on
   To a shadow

   I'm sick of love; I hear the clock tick
   This kind of love; I'm love sick

4. *Instrumental*

5. Sometimes the silence can be like the thunder
   Sometimes I wanna take to the road and plunder
   Could you ever be true?
   I think of you
   And I wonder

   I'm sick of love; I wish I'd never met you
   I'm sick of love; I'm trying to forget you

   Just don't know what to do
   I'd give anything to
   Be with you

"To think entertainers always have to be happy is a kind of shallow thing. In fact, I remember one of Bob's quotes: 'Happy? Anybody can be happy. What's the purpose of that?'"

Pete Seeger

TRYIN' TO GET TO HEAVEN

Time Out Of Mind, 1997

This was one of the songs universally acclaimed by critics after the release of 1997's *Time Out Of Mind* album. Dylan has treated his concert audiences to occasional performances, radically reworking the melody line in 2000 to stunning effect.

"What makes my songs different is that there's a foundation to them. That's why they're still around. They're not written to be performed by other people. But they're standing on a strong foundation, and subliminally that's what people are hearing."

Bob Dylan, 1997

NOT DARK YET

Time Out Of Mind, 1997

Stark and uncompromising, this deceptively gentle song was one of the key tracks on *Time Out Of Mind*, released in 1997. The album marked his second collaboration with Daniel Lanois, who had previously produced *Oh Mercy* for Dylan eight years earlier.

"I try to live within that line between despondency and hope. I'm suited to walk that line, right between the fire."

Bob Dylan, 1997

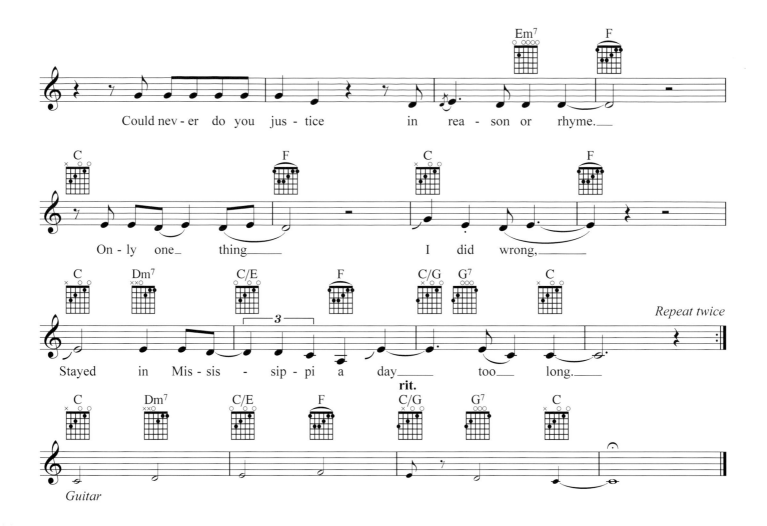

Could nev - er do you jus - tice in rea - son or rhyme.___

On - ly one___ thing___ I did wrong,___

Stayed in Mis - sis - sip - pi a day___ too___ long.___

Repeat twice

rit.

Guitar

4. Well, the devil's in the alley, mule's in the stall
   Say anything you wanna, I have heard it all
   I was thinkin' 'bout the things that Rosie said
   I was dreamin' I was sleepin' in Rosie's bed

5. Walkin' through the leaves fallin' from the trees
   Feelin' like a stranger nobody sees
   So many things that we never will undo
   I know you're sorry, I'm sorry too

   Bridge:
2. Some people will offer you their hand and some won't
   Last night I knew ya, tonight I don't
   I need somethin' strong to distract my mind
   I'm gonna look at you 'til my eyes go blind

6. Well, I got here followin' the southern star
   I crossed that river just to be where you are
   Only one thing I did wrong
   Stayed in Mississippi a day too long

7. Well, my ship's been split to splinters and it's sinkin' fast
   I'm drownin' in the poison, got no future, got no past
   But my heart is not weary, it's light and it's free
   I got nothin' but affection for all those who've sailed with me

8. Everybody movin' if they ain't already there
   Everybody got to move somewhere
   Stick with me baby, stick with me anyhow
   Things should start to get interestin' right about now

   Bridge:
3. My clothes are wet, tight on my skin
   Not as tight as the corner that I painted myself in
   I know that fortune is waitin' to be kind
   So give me your hand and say you'll be mine

9. Well, the emptiness is endless, cold as the clay
   You can always come back
        but you can't come back all the way
   Only one thing I did wrong
   Stayed in Mississippi a day too long

"It was really an honour to get to do it. You can listen to one of his songs and think it's so simple, you don't even realize how intricate it actually is – the arc of the melody, the way he uses just two or three chords but everything builds to a great release. Recording that song made me re-evaluate songwriting."

Sheryl Crow

THINGS HAVE CHANGED

🎵 *The Essential Bob Dylan, 2000*

Several Dylan songs featured prominently on the soundtrack of the 2000 movie *The Wonder Boys*, including 'Things Have Changed', newly composed for the film. The song won Dylan his first Academy Award, and he has proudly displayed the 'Oscar' as part of his stage set-up ever since. He subsequently received similar awards from the Grammy and Golden Globes judging panels.

Additional lyrics

2. This place ain't doing me any good
   I'm in the wrong town, I should be in Hollywood
   Just for a second there I thought I saw something move
   Gonna take dancing lessons do the jitterbug rag
   Ain't no shortcuts, gonna dress in drag
   Only a fool in here would think he's got anything to prove

   Bridge #2:
   Lot of water under the bridge, Lot of other stuff too
   Don't get up gentlemen, I'm only passing through

   Refrain

3. I've been walking forty miles of bad road
   If the Bible is right, the world will explode
   I've been trying to get as far away from myself as I can
   Some things are too hot to touch
   The human mind can only stand so much
   You can't win with a losing hand

   Bridge #3:
   Feel like falling in love with the first woman I meet
   Putting her in a wheel barrow and wheeling her down the street

   Refrain

4. I hurt easy, I just don't show it
   You can hurt someone and not even know it
   The next sixty seconds could be like an eternity
   Gonna get low down, gonna fly high
   All the truth in the world adds up to one big lie
   I'm in love with a woman who don't even appeal to me

   Bridge #4:
   Mr. Jinx and Miss Lucy, they jumped in the lake
   I'm not that eager to make a mistake

   Refrain

"Who knows more about being a wonder boy than Bob Dylan? He has successfully reinvented himself again and again. One of my biggest thrills as a director was the day when Bob Dylan came into the editing room and I showed him some hours of footage and talked about the imagery of the movie. He went off and wrote this fantastic song on the road using the musicians he was travelling with. He was singing about water under the bridge and many images from the movie. It was great for the movie but also a fabulous, stand-alone Bob Dylan song."

Curtis Hanson, director of *The Wonder Boys*

HIGH WATER (FOR CHARLEY PATTON)

Love And Theft, 2001

Taped during the sessions for 2001's album *Love And Theft*, a song already wrapped in foreboding took on a darker resonance after the catastrophic floods that afflicted New Orleans in 2005. Dylan dedicated the tune to Delta blues pioneer Charley Patton, who recorded a song entitled 'High Water Everywhere' in 1930.

1. I got a cravin' love for blazin' speed
   Got a hopped up Mustang Ford
   Jump into the wagon, love, throw your panties overboard
   I can write you poems, make a strong man lose his mind
   I'm no pig without a wig
   I hope you treat me kind
   Things are breakin' up out there
   High water everywhere

2. High water risin' six inches 'bove my head
   Coffins droppin' in the street
   Like balloons made out of lead
   Water pourin' into Vicksburg, don't know what I'm gonna do
   "Don't reach out for me," she said
   "Can't you see I'm drownin' too?"
   It's rough out there
   High water everywhere

3. Well, George Lewis told the Englishman, the Italian and the Jew
   "You can't open up your mind, boys
   To every conceivable point of view"
   They got Charles Darwin trapped out there on Highway Five
   Judge says to the High Sheriff
   "I want him dead or alive
   Either one, I don't care"
   High water everywhere

4. The cuckoo is a pretty bird, she warbles as she flies
   I'm preachin' the Word of God
   I'm puttin' out your eyes
   I asked Fat Nancy for somethin' to eat, she said, "Take it off the shelf
   As great as you are a man
   you'll never be greater than yourself"
   I told her I didn't really care
   High water everywhere

5. I'm gettin' up in the morning – I believe I'll dust my broom
   Keepin' away from the women
   I'm givin' 'em lots of room
   Thunder rollin' over Clarksdale, everything is lookin' blue
   I just can't be happy, love
   Unless you're happy too
   It's bad out there
   High water everywhere

"Bob Dylan! It's like trying to talk about the Pyramids. What do you do? You just stand back and… gape."

Bono

WORKINGMAN'S BLUES #2

Modern Times, 2006

As its title suggests, this highlight of Dylan's critically acclaimed *Modern Times* album from 2006 was self-consciously a sequel to an earlier song – 'Workingman's Blues', by country veteran Merle Haggard. Since the album was released, Dylan has performed the song live on several occasions.

WORKINGMAN'S BLUES #2

eve - nin' haze   set - tlin' ov - er the town,   Star light by the edge of the creek.   The
(Verses 3, 5 & 7 see block lyrics)

buy - in' power of the pro - le - tar - iat's gone down,   Mon - ey's get - tin' shal - low and weak.__   The

place I love best is a sweet mem - o - ry,   It's a new path that we trod.____   They say

low   wa - ges are a re - al - i - ty,   If we want to com - pete a - broad.____

3. Now, I'm sailin' on back, ready for the long haul
   Tossed by the winds and the seas
   I'll drag 'em all down to hell and I'll stand 'em at the wall
   I'll sell 'em to the enemies
   I'm tryin' to feed my soul with thought
   Gonna sleep off the rest of the day
   Sometimes no one wants what we got
   Sometimes you can't give it away

4. Now the place is ringed with countless foes
   Some of them may be deaf and dumb
   No man, no woman knows
   The hour that sorrow will come
   In the dark I hear the night birds call
   I can feel a lover's breath
   I sleep in the kitchen with my feet in the hall
   Sleep is like a temporary death

   Refrain

5. Well, they burned my barn and they stole my horse
   I can't save a dime
   I got to be careful, I don't want to be forced
   Into a life of continual crime
   I can see for myself that the sun is sinking
   How I wish you were here to see
   Tell me now, am I wrong in thinking
   That you have forgotten me?

6. How, they worry and they hurry and they fuss and they fret
   They waste your nights and days
   Them I will forget
   But you I'll remember always
   Old memories of you to me have clung
   You've wounded me with words
   Gonna have to straighten out your tongue
   It's all true, everything you have heard

   Refrain

7. In you, my friend, I find no blame
   Wanna look in my eyes, please do
   No one can ever claim
   That I took up arms against you
   All across the peaceful sacred fields
   They will lay you low
   They'll break your horns and slash you with steel
   I say it so it must be so

8. Now I'm down on my luck and I'm black and blue
   Gonna give you another chance
   I'm all alone, I'm expecting you
   To lead me off in a cheerful dance
   Got a brand new suit and a brand new wife
   I can live on rice and beans
   Some people never work a day in their life
   Don't know what work even means

   Refrain

"Dylan's like the Beatles or the Eiffel Tower – he's just there, his presence is so strong that you don't see him anymore."

David Gray

THUNDER ON THE MOUNTAIN

Modern Times, 2006

The opening track from the critically acclaimed 2006 album *Modern Times,* 'Thunder On The Mountain' was rapidly incorporated into his live repertoire that year, often featuring among Dylan's encores. Besides its Chuck Berry-styled structure, the song is notable for its reference to young R&B star Alicia Keys, whom Dylan had admired after seeing her on a TV awards show.

4. Thunder on the mountain, rolling like a drum
    Gonna sleep over there, that's where the music coming from
    I don't need any guide, I already know the way
    Remember this, I'm your servant both night and day

5. The pistols are poppin' and the power is down
    I'd like to try somethin', but I'm so far from town
    The sun keeps shinin' and the North Wind keeps picking up speed
    Gonna forget about myself for a while, gonna go out and see what others need

6. I've been sitting down studying the art of love
    I think it will fit me like a glove
    I want some real good woman to do just what I say
    Everybody got to wonder what's the matter with this cruel world today

7. Thunder on the mountain, rolling to the ground
    Gonna get up in the morning, walk the hard road down
    Some sweet day I'll stand beside my king
    I wouldn't betray your love or any other thing

8. Gonna raise me an army, some tough sons of bitches
    I'll recruit my army from the orphanages
    I been to St. Herman's Church and I've said my religious vows
    I've sucked the milk out of a thousand cows

9. I got the porkchops, she got the pie
    She ain't no angel and neither am I
    Shame on your greed, shame on your wicked schemes
    I'll say this, I don't give a damn about your dreams

10. Thunder on the mountain, heavy as can be
    Mean old twister bearing down on me
    All the ladies in Washington, scrambling to get out of town
    Look like something bad gonna happen, better roll your airplane down

11. Everybody's going and I want to go too
    Don't wanna take a chance with somebody new
    I did all I could, I did it right there and then
    I've already confessed- no need to confess again

12. Gonna make a lot of money, gonna go up north
    I'll plant and I'll harvest what the earth brings forth
    The hammer's on the table, the pitchfork's on the shelf
    For the love of God, you ought to take pity on yourself